Full My
One-acts
5/5
In appropriate

Social Darwinism

by Angela Gant

A SAMUEL FRENCH ACTING EDITION

SAMUEL
FRENCH
FOUNDED 1830

SAMUELFRENCH.COM

Copyright © 2012 by Angela Gant

ALL RIGHTS RESERVED

CAUTION: Professionals and amateurs are hereby warned that *SOCIAL DARWINISM* is subject to a licensing fee. It is fully protected under the copyright laws of the United States of America, the British Commonwealth, including Canada, and all other countries of the Copyright Union. All rights, including professional, amateur, motion picture, recitation, lecturing, public reading, radio broadcasting, television and the rights of translation into foreign languages are strictly reserved. In its present form the play is dedicated to the reading public only.

The amateur and professional live stage performance rights to *SOCIAL DARWINISM* are controlled exclusively by Samuel French, Inc., and licensing arrangements and performance licenses must be secured well in advance of presentation. PLEASE NOTE that amateur licensing fees are set upon application in accordance with your producing circumstances. When applying for a licensing quotation and a performance license please give us the number of performances intended, dates of production, your seating capacity and admission fee. Licensing fees are payable one week before the opening performance of the play to Samuel French, Inc., at 45 W. 25th Street, New York, NY 10010.

Licensing fee of the required amount must be paid whether the play is presented for charity or gain and whether or not admission is charged.

Professional/Stock licensing fees quoted upon application to Samuel French, Inc.

For all other rights than those stipulated above, apply to: Samuel French, Inc., 45 West 25th Street, New York, NY 10010.

Particular emphasis is laid on the question of amateur or professional readings, permission and terms for which must be secured in writing from Samuel French, Inc.

Copying from this book in whole or in part is strictly forbidden by law, and the right of performance is not transferable.

Whenever the play is produced the following notice must appear on all programs, printing and advertising for the play: "Produced by special arrangement with Samuel French, Inc."

Due authorship credit must be given on all programs, printing and advertising for the play.

ISBN 978-0-573-70063-7   Printed in U.S.A.   #28066

No one shall commit or authorize any act or omission by which the copyright of, or the right to copyright, this play may be impaired.

No one shall make any changes in this play for the purpose of production.

Publication of this play does not imply availability for performance. Both amateurs and professionals considering a production are strongly advised in their own interests to apply to Samuel French, Inc., for written permission before starting rehearsals, advertising, or booking a theatre.

No part of this book may be reproduced, stored in a retrieval system, or transmitted in any form, by any means, now known or yet to be invented, including mechanical, electronic, photocopying, recording, videotaping, or otherwise, without the prior written permission of the publisher.

MUSIC USE NOTE

Licensees are solely responsible for obtaining formal written permission from copyright owners to use copyrighted music in the performance of this play and are strongly cautioned to do so. If no such permission is obtained by the licensee, then the licensee must use only original music that the licensee owns and controls. Licensees are solely responsible and liable for all music clearances and shall indemnify the copyright owners of the play and their licensing agent, Samuel French, Inc., against any costs, expenses, losses and liabilities arising from the use of music by licensees.

IMPORTANT BILLING AND CREDIT
REQUIREMENTS

All producers of *SOCIAL DARWINISM* *must* give credit to the Author of the Play in all programs distributed in connection with performances of the Play, and in all instances in which the title of the Play appears for the purposes of advertising, publicizing or otherwise exploiting the Play and/ or a production. The name of the Author *must* appear on a separate line on which no other name appears, immediately following the title and *must* appear in size of type not less than fifty percent of the size of the title type.

SOCIAL DARWINISM opened at Texas Tech University's Lab Theatre in Lubbock, Texas on October 3, 2005. It was directed by Jeffrey Wells, assisted by Sarah S. Shaver, with scenic design by Alicia Warren, lighting by Richard Hamilton, sound by Jacob Davis, costumes by Jennifer Lara, and fight choreography by Kelly Parker. The stage manager was Carol Krueger. The cast was as follows:

ALPHA MALE . . . . Steve Wood

ALPHA FEMALE . . . . .Morgan Mercer

SUBORDINATE MALE. . . . . Adam Zarowski

SUBORDINATE FEMALE. . . . . Amanda Barnes

ADOLESCENT MALE . . . . Brice Russell

ADOLESCENT FEMALE . . . . Mary Anne Murray

OUTSIDE MALE . . . . .E. Talmadge Hill

OUTSIDE FEMALE . . . . .Kristin Abaquin

FIELD SCIENTIST. . . . . Kevin Ten Eyck

JANE . . . . .Annie Bradley

CHARACTERS

ALPHA MALE (JASON) – The strongest and oldest male; he rules by fear, money, or stature. He often cheats on his wife with the **OUTSIDE FEMALE**.

ALPHA FEMALE (ELIZABETH) – The oldest and strongest female.

SECOND BANANA (CHARLIE) – The homosexual step-brother of the **ALPHA MALE** who is always striving to move up.

SUBORDINATE FEMALE (KATE) – The most headstrong and outspoken of the women.

ADOLESCENT MALE (ISAAC) – An awkward teenager who has few social skills; he is often spurned by **ALPHA MALE**.

ADOLESCENT FEMALE (JESSIE) – A cheerleader-type of adolescent; she is not very bright, but she is her father's favorite.

OUTSIDE MALE (AUSTIN) – The sometime-lover of **SECOND BANANA**. He is an ethnicity other than Caucasian.

OUTSIDE FEMALE (MARY) – The other woman. She is an ethnicity other than Caucasian.

FIELD SCIENTIST – A male scientist studying different classes of primates. A cross between Jane Goodall and Mutual of Omaha.

JANE – Female assistant to the **FIELD SCIENTIST** who does the Field Scientist's grunt work and the tagging of the animals. She interacts with the subjects throughout the play, and is always on stage.

SETTING

The set can be sparse or elaborate, but it needs to have minimal elements of the jungle, and lower, middle, and upper classes, which can be added and/or removed.

COSTUMES

The characters can start out nude, clad in underware, or tight clothing as chimpanzees. As the characters move from rednecks, to the 1950's, and to the upper class they should add a layer of clothing until they revert to their chimpanzee form and revert to their chimp costumes.

TIME

Present.

AUTHOR'S NOTES

The **FIELD SCIENTIST**'s and **JANE**'s costumes evolve along with the other characters, and are always dressed appropriately for the class changes found within the play.

JANE "tags" some of the characters throughout the play by shooting them with a dart gun and placing an obnoxious tag over their ear that can be worn throughout the rest of the play.

ACKNOWLEDGEMENTS

Thank you to Gregg Henry, Norman Bert, Gary Garrison, Jeffrey Wells, Adam Zarowski, Eric Ruben, Connie Whitt-Lambert, Bill Untiedt, Amy Marsh, Grant Brenner, The Kennedy Center American College Theatre Festival, Texas Tech University Department of Theatre and Dance, Samuel French, and my beautiful, intellectual, talented wife and muse that I am too lucky for words to have, Jamie Hogue.

Additionally, I want to thank NYC's very own ADA Alex Spiro, Katie Doran (Advisor to the DA for LGBT issues), and Detective John Hoffman for giving me the spirit and power to make it through the judicial process, and see my assailant brought to justice. The play had already been written and produced, but may have never made it to publication. Thanks everyone!

To anyone who has ever gotten a beat down for looking like a woman, being a woman, looking like a queer, being a queer, not being manly enough, being too manly, or having the audacity to be any race other than Caucasian, here's the last laugh!

ACT I

(As the scene opens, all characters are in their under-
wear, including the **FIELD SCIENTIST,** *who is in his*
underwear and sporting a safari hat. **ALPHA MALE**
and **OUTSIDE MALE** *are absent.* **SECOND BANANA** *and*
ADOLESCENT MALE *are sparring in a jocular fashion.*
They are posturing and aware some of the females are
watching. **ALPHA FEMALE** *is grooming* **ADOLESCENT**
FEMALE *by picking lice off her back and sticking them*
in her mouth. **OUTSIDE FEMALE** *is trying to entice*
SUBORDINATE FEMALE *into eating termites with her off*
a stick. Though the **SUBORDINATE FEMALE** *is unsure*
of the **OUTSIDE FEMALE,** *she is very fond of termites.*
The **FIELD SCIENTIST** *is standing off to one side, speak-*
ing in a deep soothing voice.)

FIELD SCIENTIST. As you can see, the chimpanzees are very
much like their homo sapien cousins. Sharing ninety-
seven percent of our genetic makeup, they are the
animals most closely related to us. Over here, one can
observe two of the subordinate males defining their
status in this culture.

(SECOND BANANA *cuffs* **ADOLESCENT MALE** *in a par-*
ticularly hard-fought round.)

The adolescent male shows great courage in attack-
ing a more worthy opponent. The subordinate male is
second only to the alpha male in strength and agility,
and the adolescent male is no match.

(ADOLESCENT MALE *scampers to* **ALPHA FEMALE** *for*
protection. The **SECOND BANANA** *circles the stage area*
screaming in victory.)

FIELD SCIENTIST *(cont)*. Chimpanzee dominance is defined by their actions; the victor takes a lap around the encampment area, while the weaker of the two returns to his mother for sympathy. It is often difficult for the lowest ranking male to move up in any environment, and this one is certainly no different.

(**ALPHA FEMALE** *pushes the* **ADOLESCENT MALE** *away. He moves away to sulk in a corner by himself.*)

The alpha female realizes that, at a certain age, it is unwise for her only male child to be seen running to his mother for support. He must learn to face life and challenges on his own.

(**ADOLESCENT MALE** *simpers.*)

In short, he must learn to take it like a man.

(**SECOND BANANA** *stands and pounds his chest victorious over his weaker opponent.*)

SECOND BANANA. Hell, yeah!

FIELD SCIENTIST. Even in the animal kingdom, showboating can become excessive.

SECOND BANANA. Who's the man?

FIELD SCIENTIST. At times, much to the chagrin of the others.

SECOND BANANA. Who's the man?

(**ALPHA FEMALE** *comes up behind the* **SECOND BANANA** *and bops him on the head. The* **SECOND BANANA** *turns to retaliate, but the* **ALPHA FEMALE** *strikes a motherly pose and begins to tap her foot at him.* **SECOND BANANA** *thinks better of his attack and slowly moves away from the* **ALPHA FEMALE***, glancing sullenly back at her.* **SECOND BANANA** *then screeches at her and moves quickly to another area of the stage.*)

FIELD SCIENTIST. In a small percentage of chimpanzee cultures, the groups are run by both an alpha male and an alpha female. Unlike their more aggressive counterparts who are ruled primarily by alpha males, these groups tend to be more accepting of outsiders and less cannibalistic than their male-dominant cousins.

(ADOLESCENT MALE approaches the ADOLESCENT FEMALE and begins to show an animal interest in her.)

FIELD SCIENTIST. As in most societies, the males are more interested in mating than the females.

(ADOLESCENT FEMALE attempts to shrug off the advances of the ADOLESCENT MALE.)

In mating rituals, females only wish to mate with the highest-ranking males, and those males like to mate with as many females as they can. As in many societies, this ensures that the strongest genetic seeds are planted, so their dominant traits will continue to thrive.

(ADOLESCENT MALE attempts to hump the ADOLESCENT FEMALE and is immediately attacked by the SECOND BANANA. After successfully chasing away the ADOLESCENT MALE, the SECOND BANANA begins to show an animal interest in the ADOLESCENT FEMALE.)

The females, by instinct, shy away from lesser males, hoping for the best. They try to avoid contact with all others beneath their social class, much like many women in society today. This trend is seen by the time females reach adolescence and begin to take on certain roles within their class system.

ADOLESCENT FEMALE. *(cheerleader-like)* Yea, Team!

FIELD SCIENTIST. The males' libidos are in turn more concerned about mating than dating. Being from a highly evolved species, the athletes have a number of tactics to get the adolescent females to consent to their mating rituals.

SECOND BANANA. But if you love me, you need to show me you love me.

FIELD SCIENTIST. A great number of tactics.

SECOND BANANA. My mom is dying of cancer right now. I just need to feel safe. You want me to feel safe don't you?

FIELD SCIENTIST. But sometimes, not always the brightest tactics.

SECOND BANANA. *(indicating)* But if I don't use it, it will fall off.

(**ADOLESCENT FEMALE** *attempts to scurry away, but* **SECOND BANANA** *gives chase.*)

FIELD SCIENTIST. Some tactics, however, always work.

(**SECOND BANANA** *grabs her and begins to hump her.* **ADOLESCENT FEMALE** *tries to get away.* **SECOND BANANA** *traps her and begins to alternately fondle himself and grab at her.*)

FIELD SCIENTIST. It is possible that, in the attempt to deny the lesser male's advances, the adolescent female's rejection will only lead to a forceful reminder of a female's place in society.

(**JANE** *takes aim with her dart gun, and the* **FIELD SCIENTIST** *grabs the nose of the weapon and points it in the air.*)

Of course, we know there is no rape in the animal kingdom.

(**ADOLESCENT FEMALE** *screams.*)

And these creatures don't have feelings the way you or I do.

(**ADOLESCENT FEMALE** *cries out.* **JANE** *stalks off to her clipboard where she furiously begins to write notes.*)

Though it may be painful to watch, I assure you, these are merely animals, and in no way are they in any danger.

(**JANE** *snorts her disapproval.*)

FIELD SCIENTIST. These are the rules of their society. The subordinate male is attempting to ensure that his genetic offspring will continue on. This is important to him, since he thinks so highly of his genetic material.

(**OUTSIDE MALE** *enters and distracts the group. All characters stop what they are doing and begin to form a perimeter around the* **OUTSIDE MALE**, *moving in closer at times to get a better look or to show their dominance.* **ALPHA MALE** *begins to rise.*)

FIELD SCIENTIST. Now this is a fascinating turn of events. We don't often get to see this. When an outside male comes in contact with a pre-existing chimpanzee group, any number of things can happen. Let's watch closely as the events unfold.

(The **ALPHA MALE,** *now clear-headed, moves in and immediately takes charge. He is wearing a necklace that befits his position as alpha male. The* **FIELD SCIENTIST** *indicates the situation to* **JANE,** *who moves in as well, careful to avoid the other characters.)*

As we can see, the alpha male has just returned to find the newcomer in his presence. Indeed, if this were completely an alpha male-driven society, no doubt the outside male chimpanzee would be killed outright and eaten for his succulent meat. Look at the alpha male immediately take charge of the situation. This is one of the attributes that separate the alpha male from the lesser males.

(The **ALPHA MALE** *attacks the* **OUTSIDE MALE,** *toying with him. The* **OUTSIDE MALE** *cowers.)*

In chimpanzee societies, which are controlled by both alpha males and alpha females, the group has a tendency to be more tolerant of outsiders. Unfortunately for the outside male, that does not necessarily ensure his survival at this critical juncture. These animals are still very wary of those trying to encroach on their pack.

(The other characters move off from their tight perimeter, except for the **ALPHA FEMALE,** *to give the* **ALPHA MALE** *room to investigate. The* **SECOND BANANA** *is the last to leave, giving the* **OUTSIDE MALE** *a parting shot as he crosses the stage.)*

Actually, an interesting note on this particular group is that they have already accepted an outside female. If you look past the others, she is the one always more separate from the group. Still, it is not the same as taking in a male outsider.

*(The **OUTSIDE MALE** cowers.)*

The outside male must be very desperate and hungry to attempt to enter this pack. No doubt, there is some reason why he was forced out or lost from his previous pack. The alpha male has a lot to consider here. He must consider not only the well being of his pack, but also consider whether or not he wants to be responsible for another adult male individual.

*(The **ALPHA MALE** circles the **OUTSIDE MALE**, who has taken a submissive posture.)*

It's very important at this juncture for the outside male to show his submissiveness to the alpha male here. He's certainly not small for a chimpanzee, and he's trying to make himself appear even smaller and less of a threat to increase his chance for survival and his admission into the new group.

*(The **SECOND BANANA** moves in too close to the perimeter laid out by the **ALPHA MALE**.)*

Oop. The subordinate male is encroaching a little too much on the alpha male's investigative territory.

*(The **ALPHA MALE** responds in a dominant manner, but the **SECOND BANANA** is slow to retreat.)*

The subordinate male gets the warning from the alpha male to move off, and he does, but he's responding really slowly here. It's not a good tactic for the subordinate male. The alpha male isn't going to appreciate that.

*(The **ALPHA MALE** cuffs him and sends him rolling.)*

The subordinate male is going to try to cry foul here, and you can tell he wants to come up swinging.

*(The **SECOND BANANA** pulls out a penalty flag and throws it to the ground. He jumps up and down, pointing to the flag.)*

The penalty flag really not going to do him any good here. It's considered fair play in the society where he is always relegated to second banana. Remember, the alpha male is an alpha male for a reason. This could be a really dumb play here on the part of the subordinate male.

(The **SECOND BANANA** *stands upright in a threatening manner. The* **ALPHA MALE** *stands to his full height.* **SECOND BANANA** *thinks better of it and crosses away. The* **ADOLESCENT MALE** *points and laughs.)*

Probably wise for him to back off at this moment. Not a good time to challenge the alpha male with an outsider present.

(The **SECOND BANANA** *cuffs the* **ADOLESCENT MALE** *as he passes by him. The* **ADOLESCENT MALE** *crosses to the penalty flag and picks it up, shaking it in the* **SECOND BANANA**'s *face.)*

You'd think the adolescent male would have learned from his experience, but he's really not that bright.

*(***SECOND BANANA** *takes the flag from the* **ADOLESCENT MALE** *and shoves it in the* **ADOLESCENT MALE**'s *screaming mouth.)*

The subordinate male isn't going to let him get away with much right now; he's got to save face from the ego bruising he just received from the alpha male.

(The **ALPHA MALE** *moves over to the* **SECOND BANANA** *and the* **ADOLESCENT MALE** *to quiet them down, and the two of them scamper in opposite directions. The* **ALPHA MALE** *follows the* **ADOLESCENT MALE** *and pulls the flag out of his mouth.)*

ALPHA MALE. Boy, what's wrong with you?

(The **ALPHA FEMALE** *moves in and begins to sniff the* **OUTSIDE MALE**.)*

FIELD SCIENTIST. It looks like the alpha female has begun to show an interest in the newcomer. This appears to soothe the sometimes-volatile alpha male.

(The **ALPHA FEMALE** *begins to poke at the* **OUTSIDE MALE**.)*

She could be a real lifesaver here. With all the commotion, the alpha male is unlikely to accept the outside male unless the alpha female gives her approval.

(The **ALPHA FEMALE** *begins to hump the* **OUTSIDE MALE**.*)*

In the chimpanzee world, the alpha male and alpha female show their acceptance of an outsider by humping him. *(excited)* In human society, it's something one might find at a swinger's bar. These types of bars of course come in many varieties. My favorite is more of an upper class bump and grind.

*(***JANE** *clears her throat.)*

But I digress...

ALPHA MALE. You like this one, Ma?

*(***ALPHA FEMALE** *is still humping the* **OUTSIDE MALE**.*)*

ALPHA FEMALE. He smells real nice, Pa.

(They revert to their chimpanzee form and the **ALPHA MALE** *moves in for a closer look at the* **OUTSIDE MALE**, *who remains perfectly docile.* **ALPHA MALE** *looks at* **ALPHA FEMALE**, *sighs, and quickly humps the* **OUTSIDE MALE** *and then moves off.)*

FIELD SCIENTIST. Once the alpha male has accepted the outside male, he will now pretend not to notice him. The outside male has been established now as the lowest ranking adult male of the group. More than likely, the adolescent male will one day hold the pre-eminent position of becoming the alpha male of the group, since he is the first-born male offspring of the alpha male.

*(***ADOLESCENT MALE** *picks his butt and sniffs his finger.)*

Well—maybe.

*(***ADOLESCENT MALE** *sticks his finger in his mouth. One by one, the individual chimpanzees approach the* **OUTSIDE MALE**.*)*

All the chimpanzees move in for a closer look, barring the alpha male and alpha female, who have already granted their approval.

(The females move in first. The **OUTSIDE FEMALE** *moves away first. The* **ALPHA MALE** *shows an interest in her.)*

In the two years we've been studying this group the alpha male has always shown an affinity for the outside female over any other female of his group. Though none could deny him, he prefers a taste of foreign flesh. The alpha female, who is rightfully his mate, accepts his philandering, as it were. Of course, in this society there is no true monogamy, so henceforth, there is no cause for her to be jealous.

(The **ADOLESCENT MALE,** *now no longer the lowest ranking male, sticks his hands down his pants and flings feces on the* **OUTSIDE MALE.** *The* **SUBORDINATE FEMALE,** *irritated by the poo-flinging, hurls some back at him and scampers off.)*

The adolescent male, now excited to no longer be the lowest ranking male, flings his excrement in delight, though not everyone is as excited by it as he is.

(The **ADOLESCENT MALE** *takes a victory lap.* **SECOND BANANA** *moves up behind the* **OUTSIDE MALE** *and sucker punches him, then slowly moves off.)*

The attack by the subordinate male is merely to show his strength and authority.

*(***SUBORDINATE FEMALE** *approaches* **OUTSIDE MALE** *who shies away.)*

You can see here that the subordinate female wants to help, but in a society relegated to nonverbal communication her intentions are unclear to the outside male.

*(***SUBORDINATE FEMALE** *approaches again and the* **OUTSIDE MALE** *shies away.)*

Of course one can hardly blame him after his official welcoming.

*(*SUBORDINATE FEMALE *approaches and the* OUTSIDE MALE *postures to attack.)*

She's got to be careful here. Animals are most dangerous when they are wounded and confused. If only they had the ability to communicate verbally, her intentions would be made clear to him. Then perhaps these kinds of misunderstandings could be avoided.

SUBORDINATE FEMALE. I just want to help you. Won't you let me help you?

*(*OUTSIDE MALE *sniffs her hand and moves closer. A clock begins to chime.* SECOND BANANA *approaches the* OUTSIDE MALE *again, this time giving him a wedgie. Everyone giggles, except for the* ALPHA FEMALE *and the* SUBORDINATE FEMALE, *who show signs of disapproval.)*

Times do change, and people change with the times. At least that's what many would have us believe. But does time really affect the animal kingdom in a traditional way?

(The clock strikes two. SUBORDINATE FEMALE *puts on skirt and approaches the* OUTSIDE MALE *pulling on a sweater. She picks up the penalty flag and begins to wipe off the feces.)*

SUBORDINATE FEMALE. Who did this to you? Talk to me. You can tell me, you know. You'll be safe here.

*(*ALPHA MALE *pulls on a wife beater and, one by one, the characters begin to put on a single layer of clothing and animate from their chimpanzee mode to their redneck society mode. The* FIELD SCIENTIST *adds on khakis and a shirt.)*

ALPHA MALE. Kate, will you leave the boy alone? He probably don't wanna talk about it, 'specially to a girl. Somebody shows up covered in shit, they generally don't wanna discuss it. Well, how'd you get covered in shit, there, boy? I guaran—fuckin'—tee you, nobody really wants to know the answer to that, 'ceptin' you.

FIELD SCIENTIST. The alpha male was considerate enough to let the outsider, at least temporarily, reside in his family unit. But much to his exasperation and chagrin, the outside male is pulling too much of his pack's focus.

SUBORDINATE FEMALE. You could at least try to be considerate of his feelings. He does have feelings, you know.

(The **ALPHA MALE** *sighs and walks off.)*

FIELD SCIENTIST. A smart leader knows when to allow a member of his pack a bit of latitude in dealing with unusual circumstances.

ALPHA MALE. *(to* **ADOLESCENT MALE***)* Boy, go get me another beer.

*(***ADOLESCENT MALE** *stares at him and squeals in a chimpanzee fashion, bobbing up and down.)*

Boy, I said go get me another beer.

*(***ALPHA MALE** *picks up* **ADOLESCENT MALE** *by his ear.* **ADOLESCENT MALE** *squeals in a chimp voice and tries to get away.)*

Don't you back talk me, boy. If you don't quit that mamby-pambying around. I'll tan that hide of yours, so help me God.

*(***ADOLESCENT MALE** *scampers off in a chimpanzee fashion.)*

It's all your doin'. It's all your damn motherin' him that's done it. How's he gonna grow up to take over this place when he ain't much better than a girl?

*(***ALPHA FEMALE** *screams and runs up to him on all fours. She pounds at his chest and returns to her original position.)*

Goddammit, woman, I done told you not to do that again. You will respect me in this house.

*(***ALPHA FEMALE** *blows him a kiss.)*

ALPHA MALE. *(cont.)* Don't be getting' all sweet on me nei-
ther. I know your feminine wiles and how they work.
It was enough for us to get hitched and for you to get
three kids out of the bargain, but that's where it ends.
A man has needs. I got an itch, and sometimes I just
gots to scratch it…

(**ALPHA MALE** *hugs* **OUTSIDE FEMALE.**)

Ain't that right, baby?

(**ALPHA FEMALE** *gives him a raspberry, does a back-
wards roll, and gives him the "fuck off" hand and fist
motion.* **SECOND BANANA** *puts on a denim shirt, which
he leaves open.*)

SECOND BANANA. I certainly wouldn't let no woman talk to
me like that.

ALPHA MALE. Well little brother, I don't see you havin' no
woman to complain about.

(**ALPHA MALE** *is still hugging* **OUTSIDE FEMALE.**)

SUBORDINATE FEMALE. Why is she here anyway? Everyone
will be over in a few hours. You could be a little respect-
ful, if not of Mama, at least of the rest of us.

SECOND BANANA. Don't bother me none.

SUBORDINATE FEMALE. That's because you have the moral
standards of an animal.

SECOND BANANA. Lordy, one semester of junior college
and don't you talk pretty?

SUBORDINATE FEMALE. You have no idea what I just said,
do you?

(**OUTSIDE MALE** *laughs.*)

SECOND BANANA. What are you laughin' at, boy? You show
up, covered in shit or somethin', and you think you're
gonna laugh at me? Fuckin' retard, you probably can't
even talk. Can you talk, 'tard? Or did they cut out your
tongue? Maybe I'll cut it out for ya.

FIELD SCIENTIST. The subordinate male cannot let the challenge to his authority go by without confronting his
giggling attacker. Males in this species are extremely
afraid of losing face in front of their peers.

(**SUBORDINATE FEMALE** *wipes the dirty flag on the* **SECOND BANANA***'s face.*)

SUBORDINATE FEMALE. Here, you got something on your face. Let me clean it off for you...

SECOND BANANA. Bitch, I'll kill you! Don't touch me with that shit-covered rag!

ALPHA MALE. That's enough!

SUBORDINATE FEMALE. Guess he told you.

ALPHA MALE. *(to* **SUBORDINATE FEMALE***)* I said that's enough.

FIELD SCIENTIST. In a complex social structure there are many rules. Though a father will protect his daughter, even an adopted one, he cannot stand by and allow a mere lowly ranked female to repeatedly attack a male.

SUBORDINATE FEMALE. But Dad...

ADOLESCENT FEMALE. You know Daddy's always right.

ALPHA MALE. That's my baby girl.

ADOLESCENT FEMALE. I love you, Daddy.

ALPHA MALE. *(coddling* **ADOLESCENT FEMALE***)* That's why you're my little pumpkin head.

(**ADOLESCENT MALE** *enters with enough beer for all the males, excluding the* **OUTSIDE MALE***. All other characters begin to dress and speak as rednecks.*)

ALPHA MALE. Personally, I think she's sweet on ya.

SUBORDINATE FEMALE. Dad.

ALPHA MALE. I'm just sayin', ya'll act just like your ma and me when we first got together.

ALPHA FEMALE. That was a long time ago.

ALPHA MALE. It took me a while to learn you right. *(flexing his muscle)* But you learned, didn't ya?

ALPHA FEMALE. If you want to call it learnin'.

ALPHA MALE. Weren't my fault you were a slow learner. Some lessons are worth repeating.

ADOLESCENT FEMALE. Why does everyone always have to fight?

SECOND BANANA. All right pretty lady, I'll make you a deal. You agree to go to the dance with me tomorrow night, and I'll be sweet as can be. I'll be on my best behavior for you… I might even take bath.

SUBORDINATE FEMALE. That's sick. He's our uncle.

SECOND BANANA. We ain't blood related, so what's it to you? Why don't you mind your own fuckin' business?

ALPHA FEMALE. I won't have you using that language in the house.

SECOND BANANA. We ain't in the house proper, now are we? *(noticing* **OUTSIDE MALE***)* Why is that 'tard still here?

SUBORDINATE FEMALE. Because for some reason or another, no one will ask you to leave.

*(***SECOND BANANA*** backhands her.)*

OUTSIDE FEMALE. Leave her be. You ain't nothin' but a bully.

ALPHA MALE. Everything's all right.

SECOND BANANA. Happy now?

*(***OUTSIDE MALE*** stands up.)*

Whatever you're thinking about, 'tard, I'd sit my ass back down if I was you.

ADOLESCENT FEMALE. Look, I'll go to the dance with you just leave her alone.

ALPHA FEMALE. You don't have to if you don't want to.

SUBORDINATE FEMALE. *(under her breath)* Way to take one for the team.

ADOLESCENT MALE. *(aloud)* Way to take one for the team.

SECOND BANANA. You watch your mouth, boy. You know I can kick your ass. Is that what you want?

ALPHA MALE. Drink your beer and go cool off.

*(***ADOLESCENT MALE*** takes a magnifying glass and begins trying to burn bugs while sitting open legged on the ground.)*

SECOND BANANA. That boy's mouth of his is going to get his ass in trouble.

(FIELD SCIENTIST *indicates to "tag"* ADOLESCENT FEMALE, *which* JANE *does, though the other characters do not notice.*)

ALPHA MALE. And I said, drink your beer and go cool off.

FIELD SCIENTIST. *(standing by felled* ADOLESCENT FEMALE *though* JANE *is doing all the work)* It's of the utmost importance to track these animals' movements to see how they progress through their lives. As soon as the quick acting tranquilizer wears off she will be as good as new.

(FIELD SCIENTIST *slaps* ADOLESCENT FEMALE *as though she were a head of cattle.*)

It can be quite dangerous out here in the wild. *(full of himself)* One must always be aware of ones surroundings and take every precaution; one never knows the danger that might befall one.

(JANE *is openly staring at him.* FIELD SCIENTIST *sees her and turns around quickly.*)

Good job, Jane.

ALPHA FEMALE. *(to* SUBORDINATE FEMALE*)* Are you all right? You want me to get you a cold washrag?

SUBORDINATE FEMALE. I'm fine.

ALPHA FEMALE. You know you can't go mouthin' off to the men-folk that way. I brung you up better than that.

SUBORDINATE FEMALE. It's just not right.

ALPHA FEMALE. It's the way things are. You can't just go changin' things to suit yourself. I don't want you to have to learn things the way I did. Here, we can go have a lie down for a minute. You'll feel better.

SUBORDINATE FEMALE. I said I was fine. *(pause)* I'm sorry, Mama. Really I'm fine.

SECOND BANANA. If you'd watch that mouth of yours, you might have a date for the spring dance too.
Maybe the 'tard will take you.

ALPHA FEMALE. *(to* **OUTSIDE MALE***)* Tell you the truth, the spring dance is about the biggest thing around these parts.

*(***ADOLESCENT FEMALE*** rouses herself.* **ADOLESCENT MALE** *continues burning bugs with a magnifying glass.* **ADOLESCENT FEMALE** *begins playing with cat's cradle.)*

FIELD SCIENTIST. The spring dance is the rite of youth, and often involves the rituals in finding a mate.

ALPHA FEMALE. That's how I ended up with that big lug there.

ALPHA MALE. Yeah, there's nothin' more romantic than tryin' to get it on while every mosquito in the county is trying to munch on your dick.

ALPHA FEMALE. What have I told you about that kind of talk?

ALPHA MALE. What? I can't say mosquitoes?

ALPHA FEMALE. Especially in front of company...

SECOND BANANA. Company, what company? Some mute retard? He's probably got some retard disease, gonna infect us all and make us dumb.

SUBORDINATE FEMALE. I think you caught it.

ADOLESCENT MALE. Maybe you done caught it.

SECOND BANANA. Dammit, boy.

ADOLESCENT FEMALE. You promised.

ALPHA MALE. Son, I just don't know what to do with you. Son, are you listenin'?

ADOLESCENT MALE. Dad, I gotta go to the bathroom.

ALPHA MALE. Boy, what's wrong with you? Just go! Hell, you got a dick and there's a tree.

ALPHA FEMALE. Jase, really, is that necessary?

ALPHA MALE. Well what the hell is wrong with that boy? Are you sure he's mine?

ALPHA FEMALE. Any more talk like that and it's going to be more than mosquitoes that go after that prick of yours.

FIELD SCIENTIST. Though these antics may seem dangerous, this is a very old game the alpha female and alpha male are playing.

ALPHA MALE. And she wonders why I have to find relief somewhere else...

SECOND BANANA. *(to* **ADOLESCENT FEMALE***)* So, we're going to the dance together, huh? I expect you to look real pretty for me. You got a new dress, right? I'd like to see you in something new, something skimpy.

(**SECOND BANANA** *sniffs* **ADOLESCENT FEMALE**.*)*

SUBORDINATE FEMALE. And you wonder why your last girlfriend didn't stick around. *(to* **OUTSIDE MALE***)* She was weird anyway. She would only eat food out of this suitcase. If you gave her food, she's put it in the suitcase. If you ask me, she was about half retarded herself.

SECOND BANANA. She didn't mean nothin' to me anyway.

ADOLESCENT FEMALE. *(to* **SECOND BANANA***)* You seemed sweet on her at the time.

ADOLESCENT MALE. You liked the suitcase girl.

SECOND BANANA. *(to* **ALPHA MALE***)* You've got the mouthiest group of women over here I've ever seen.

(**SECOND BANANA** *spits near/at* **JANE**.*)*

Why don't you do something about your mouthy women folk?

(**JANE** *starts to react and the* **FIELD SCIENTIST**, *oblivious, pulls her to him.)*

FIELD SCIENTIST. Let's watch closely as the subordinate male tries to subtly undermine the authority of the alpha male. The alpha male must protect his flock of women that the subordinate male would seek to covet. Let's watch and see how the situation unfolds.

ALPHA MALE. Why, they don't give me no trouble. If they respect ya, they don't cause you no real trouble. If you catch my meaning.

SECOND BANANA. You trying to say something?

FIELD SCIENTIST. This could be construed as a direct challenge to the alpha male. Let's see if he perceives it that way…

ALPHA MALE. Boy, you're getting' a little close to my space here. I'd ratchet down if I's you.

FIELD SCIENTIST. I think we have a definite affirmative to that challenge.

(**JANE** *shushes the* **FIELD SCIENTIST** *while the* **ALPHA MALE** *and* **SECOND BANANA** *begin to circle each other. Clock ticking begins in the background.*)

SECOND BANANA. I don't know who you think died and left you in charge, but I can do 'bout anything you can do.

ALPHA MALE. That right?

SECOND BANANA. You're startin' to get a little older now. Not quite as fast, maybe not quite as strong.

ALPHA MALE. Think so?

SECOND BANANA. Me, I'm in my prime.

ALPHA MALE. You think you can take me, huh?

SECOND BANANA. Maybe.

ALPHA MALE. Just like that?

SECOND BANANA. Just like that.

FIELD SCIENTIST. This particular alpha male usually waits for the aggressor to attack, giving him every opportunity to avoid the confrontation.

(**SECOND BANANA** *swings his beer bottle at the head of the* **ALPHA MALE,** *almost hitting* **JANE**. *The* **ALPHA MALE** *deftly avoids it and they begin to spar.*)

ALPHA MALE. C'mon boy. Let's see what you've got.

(**SECOND BANANA** *scores a few punches and a few bites. The* **ALPHA MALE** *bides his time, letting the* **SECOND BANANA** *move in closer.*)

FIELD SCIENTIST. The alpha male is going to attempt to draw him in closer. He's definitely drawing him in. The only question is whether the alpha male will go for the serious injury on the subordinate male or…

(**ALPHA MALE** *dodges a swing and takes the* **SECOND BANANA** *by the ear.*)

No, he's going for the humiliation factor here. You've really got to watch your ears; this alpha male is quite a character.

ALPHA MALE. I've had just about enough of you for one evening, boy.

SECOND BANANA. Fuck you.

ALPHA MALE. *(wrenching him harder)* Maybe I didn't hear you correctly. Or maybe you didn't hear me correctly. I said, I've had about enough of you for one evening.

SECOND BANANA. And I said, fuck you.

(**SECOND BANANA** *throws penalty flag.* **ADOLESCENT MALE** *picks it up, giggling, and ties it on as a headband and runs around.*)

ALPHA MALE. *(wrenching him harder still)* Say that one more time. I'm waiting.

SECOND BANANA. Sorry.

ALPHA MALE. What's that?

SECOND BANANA. I said I was sorry.

ALPHA MALE. Louder.

SECOND BANANA. Sorry.

(**ALPHA MALE** *releases* **SECOND BANANA** *who appears to consider a second attack on the* **ALPHA MALE** *and then reconsiders it.* **ADOLESCENT MALE** *grabs four beers and passes them out to the males.*)

ALPHA MALE. That a boy. I might learn you yet.

SECOND BANANA. *(indicating to* **OUTSIDE MALE,** *who is getting a beer)* Why the hell does he get a beer? What the hell has he done? Just some no-name retard that wanders in off the street, and we're gonna give him a beer?

ADOLESCENT MALE. We've got enough for everybody.

SECOND BANANA. They teach you that in school?

ALPHA MALE. Let him be. That was real considerate of you, son. Kinda dumb, but real nice.

(*The* **ADOLESCENT MALE** *beams in pride.*)

ADOLESCENT MALE. I'm considerate.

SUBORDINATE FEMALE. Why do you care about him so much? He's not hurtin' anything. Hell, he's not doing anything but sitting there bleeding.

SECOND BANANA. Bleedin'? He's probably one of those AIDS faggots; I say we get rid of his ass right now. He's probably infecting all of us as we speak.

SUBORDINATE FEMALE. That's just stupid. He's not hurtin' you.

SECOND BANANA. He is if he gets me sick. What if he gets us all sick? You can't just bring home every mangy dog you find.

ADOLESCENT MALE. He's not a dog, though. He's a man.

SECOND BANANA. Anybody that looks like that has got to be part animal.

ADOLESCENT FEMALE. You promised, you remember, you said…

SUBORDINATE FEMALE. Why don't you go get drunk and pass out somewhere else?

SECOND BANANA. You're some kinda faggot lover, ain't ya? That it? Faggot lover.

FIELD SCIENTIST. Not feeling particularly physically inspired at the moment, the subordinate male is reduced to name-calling.

SECOND BANANA. Faggot lover.

SUBORDINATE FEMALE. I'd say it takes one to know one.

ALPHA FEMALE. Why don't we all go inside for a little while? I think the heat's starting to get to everyone.

SECOND BANANA. What are you trying to say?

ADOLESCENT MALE. (*trying to be helpful*) She said, it takes one to know one.

ALPHA MALE. Son.

SECOND BANANA. I've had just about enough of your mouth.

ALPHA FEMALE. Kate, we've talked about this before.

OUTSIDE FEMALE. Just ignore him. You know how he gets. He's just trying to get all the attention.

ADOLESCENT FEMALE. Why does everyone have to fight all the time? You promised you wouldn't do this.

SECOND BANANA. I'm not doing anything. I'm just having a little conversation here is all.

ADOLESCENT FEMALE. I hate this.

ALPHA MALE. If you get scared just come over here by me, little pumpkin head.

(**ALPHA FEMALE** *starts to swoon and catches herself.*)

ALPHA MALE. Dammit Ma, what's wrong with you?

ADOLESCENT FEMALE. Mama, are you okay?

OUTSIDE FEMALE. *(to* **ADOLESCENT FEMALE***)* You win if you walk away, you know. You'll be the bigger person for it. Just let it go.

ALPHA MALE. Just trying to get attention, aren't you Ma?

ALPHA FEMALE. Don't you worry your pretty little head about it, dear. Just one of my spells.

SUBORDINATE FEMALE. I can protect myself just fine.

ALPHA MALE. Spells my ass. I'm getting sick of your spells woman.

OUTSIDE FEMALE. He could really hurt you.

ALPHA FEMALE. It's nothing. Won't happen again.

ALPHA MALE. Better not.

OUTSIDE FEMALE. I just don't want to see you hurt. Let me help you.

SUBORDINATE FEMALE. I don't need your type of help. The only person around here you can help is Dad. Why don't you just keep in mind what you are around here.

ADOLESCENT MALE. Don't get hurt, Kate. I don't want you to get hurt. Dad?

ALPHA MALE. Your sister's gotta learn, boy.

SECOND BANANA. Well, well, well. Seems like everyone's scared for ya. Are you smart enough to be scared with all your college smarts? Are you gonna try to protect that faggot retard of yours?

SUBORDINATE FEMALE. You're nothing but a homophobic bully.

SECOND BANANA. Yeah well… what'd you call me?

ALPHA MALE. Learned that in college, did ya? 'Bout them homosexuals. I've heard some of the learnin' that goes on in college, 'specially 'tween the women-folk. Maybe I shoulda gone to college myself.

ALPHA FEMALE. I think you've learned enough on your own. I've seen those magazines of yours.

ALPHA MALE. They're pretty good, ain't they? Why can't ya'll do stuff like that?

SECOND BANANA. You think I'm some kinda… funny bunny?

SUBORDINATE FEMALE. I like rump ranger. Even butt pirate's got a nice ring to it.

(**OUTSIDE MALE** *stands.*)

SECOND BANANA. What'd you say, bitch?

SUBORDINATE FEMALE. Faggot.

SECOND BANANA. Bitch, it's time somebody in this family taught you some manners.

(**SECOND BANANA** *pulls back to hit* **SUBORDINATE FEMALE**, *but* **OUTSIDE MALE** *grabs his wrist.*)

OUTSIDE MALE. Once is enough.

SECOND BANANA. So you can talk, retard.

(**SECOND BANANA** *and* **OUTSIDE MALE** *begin to sniff and circle each other.*)

FIELD SCIENTIST. Having his use of power curtailed by the lowest ranking male is not acceptable. The outside male may have just overstepped his bounds by interfering. Let us observe the confrontation as it unfolds…

(**FIELD SCIENTIST** *goes to* **JANE** *and whispers in her ear.*)

OUTSIDE MALE. Yeah, I can still talk. Are you scared?

SECOND BANANA. What, of some little bitch dog like you? I'm looking forward to this.

OUTSIDE MALE. Me too.

(**OUTSIDE MALE** *swoons and almost falls.* **SECOND BANANA** *laughs.*)

SUBORDINATE FEMALE. Leave him alone. Can't you see he's sick?

SECOND BANANA. Sick with AIDS. Ain't that right, faggot?

(**OUTSIDE MALE** *and* **SECOND BANANA** *begin to circle each other like wrestlers.* **JANE** *rings bell three times for live sound effect.*)

FIELD SCIENTIST. *(transforming voice into more of a wrestling announcer Howard Cosell crossover. Anytime* **JANE** *tries to speak, the* **FIELD SCIENTIST** *cuts her off.)* This is the confrontation we've been waiting for. The outside male now has the opportunity to show his stuff, what he's made of, if you will.

OUTSIDE MALE. *(to* **SUBORDINATE FEMALE***)* It'll be okay.

(*The characters circle around them and begin to cheer. They form a wrestling ring around the* **SECOND BANANA** *and the* **OUTSIDE MALE***. The characters begin to take on more chimpanzee-like behavior as they become engrossed in the conflict. The* **ALPHA MALE** *stands to his full height and pounds his chest. The* **ALPHA MALE** *circles the two contestants on his knuckles and then takes his place in the middle of the ring as the referee.*)

FIELD SCIENTIST. The subordinate male definitely has the upper hand, but really it could be anybody's win here. I've got to be real honest with you; this battle is of the utmost importance to the subordinate male. He's definitely in better physical condition than the challenger, but he has got to win here. If he loses here today, it's all over for him. There are no playoffs, there is no extended season, this is it for the second strongest male.

(*All dialogue held between the* **SECOND BANANA** *and the* **OUTSIDE MALE** *is not heard by the other characters.*)

There's no turning back at this point.

SECOND BANANA. Faggot.

OUTSIDE MALE. That's kinda funny coming from you.

> (**SECOND BANANA** *sucker punches* **OUTSIDE MALE** *who goes back "into the ropes." The* **OUTSIDE MALE** *rushes out only to be "clotheslined" by the* **SECOND BANANA**. *A crowd is heard cheering.*)

FIELD SCIENTIST. I'm telling you, this guy really knows how to put on a show. He's always been a big crowd pleaser. He's the guy you love to hate. They're absolutely eating this up.

> (**OUTSIDE MALE** *gets up unnoticed while the* **SECOND BANANA** *is showboating.* **OUTSIDE MALE** *hits him on the back of the head. The* **SECOND BANANA** *turns and they begin to grapple.*)

SECOND BANANA. You can't beat me.

OUTSIDE MALE. We'll see about that.

SECOND BANANA. You haven't forgotten about last night have you, lover?

OUTSIDE MALE. There were three of you last night.

SECOND BANANA. And you enjoyed taking every one of us, didn't you, faggot?

OUTSIDE MALE. You're the one fucking a guy and I'm the faggot?

SECOND BANANA. You know you wanted it. You know you loved it. Felt good, didn't it?

FIELD SCIENTIST. It would be interesting if we could understand their exact communications to each other. Half this competition is mental and the other half is physical. You really have to master both sides to come out victorious.

SECOND BANANA. You know you wanted it.

OUTSIDE MALE. What would your friends think? What would your family think if I told them what got you off?

SECOND BANANA. *(putting* **OUTSIDE MALE** *in a headlock)* If you ever breathe a word about it to anyone, you'll have seen your last day. I'll kill you, you hear me boy? You'll rue the day.

(**OUTSIDE MALE** *gets away and pins the* **SECOND BANANA** *for a two count.*)

FIELD SCIENTIST. This is definitely an exciting turn of events here. It seems our newcomer has a great deal more stamina than anyone would have imagined. Simply incredible.

OUTSIDE MALE. Did you enjoy that? How did that make you feel?

SECOND BANANA. You're nothing to me.

FIELD SCIENTIST. That was a dangerous moment for the subordinate male. A lot is riding on this; he can't let himself get pinned like that so early on. You can see that it has really shaken his confidence.

SECOND BANANA. How long do you think you can last out here, boy?

OUTSIDE MALE. Long enough.

FIELD SCIENTIST. There's still a lot more fight, but you can see the outside male is getting tired. The subordinate male is starting to wear him down. It's a tough call here.

(**SECOND BANANA** *begins to listen to the* **FIELD SCIENTIST** *and is getting agitated by his comments.*)

Ohhh, one more second on a pin like that, and it's a complete loss of status for the subordinate male. That would leave him with a loss of face that could drag him all the way to the bottom.

(*The* **FIELD SCIENTIST** *continues as the* **SECOND BANANA** *crosses out of the ring and begins to head for his position. The* **SECOND BANANA** *enters into his chimpanzee form.* **JANE** *sees him coming and steps out of the way.*)

He would become the lowest ranking male. I just don't see how he could ever recover from that. It would be a heavy loss indeed.

(The **SECOND BANANA** *attacks the* **FIELD SCIENTIST***, who drops the microphone and manages to get away from the* **SECOND BANANA***. The* **SECOND BANANA** *returns to the ring and the* **FIELD SCIENTIST** *goes back to his regular monologue voice.)*

FIELD SCIENTIST. *(cont.)* That was a close one. It can be quite dangerous out here. You never know when one of these animals is going to turn on you and attack. After a while, they're usually dulled to our existence, but as you can clearly see, this is a dangerous environment, and anything can happen.

*(***JANE** *rolls her eyes and sighs.)*

SECOND BANANA. Now to deal with you.

FIELD SCIENTIST. *(back to his wrestling announcer voice)* That little stunt certainly isn't going to do him any good. Though it's a crowd pleaser, it certainly isn't going to take any of the pressure off him to win this battle.

SECOND BANANA. C'mon boy, you want you some of this?

OUTSIDE MALE. You can't treat people the way you do.

SECOND BANANA. People yeah, but you're not quite people, now, are you? Retard. Faggot. What you got to say for yourself?

OUTSIDE MALE. This, big boy.

*(***OUTSIDE MALE** *comes up and kisses* **SECOND BANANA***.)*

FIELD SCIENTIST. This battle has just taken a turn for the weird. For some reason or another, the outside male has just kissed the subordinate male. You heard me right, folks, he just kissed him right there in the ring.

*(***SUBORDINATE FEMALE** *enters the ring with a folding chair and hits the* **SECOND BANANA** *on the back of the head.)*

FIELD SCIENTIST. Seems as though we're going to have some audience participation this evening.

(**ALPHA MALE** *chases* **SUBORDINATE FEMALE** *out of the ring, and the wrestlers begin again, first with the* **OUTSIDE MALE** *getting the upper hand and then the* **SECOND BANANA** *taking control again.*)

FIELD SCIENTIST. This battle could go either way, with dominance hanging in the balance. Who will go on? Who will be victorious?

(**OUTSIDE MALE** *pins* **SECOND BANANA** *for a two count.* **SECOND BANANA** *immediately recovers.*)

FIELD SCIENTIST. You can tell both the combatants are getting physically and emotionally drained.

(*The* **ALPHA MALE** *trips up* **OUTSIDE MALE** *and the* **SECOND BANANA** *jumps on him holding him for a questionable three count.* **SECOND BANANA** *holds up his hands victorious, and the "ring" remains intact through the next section of dialogue.*)

ALPHA MALE. *(aside to* **OUTSIDE MALE***)* Sorry, boy, I couldn't let you beat him like that. It would've hurt him in ways that it couldn't hurt you. Bein' a man is all he got.

SECOND BANANA. *(yelling at* **OUTSIDE MALE***)* How do you like that, retard?

ALPHA MALE. You'll go back to wherever you're from, and you'll be fine, but he ain't never leavin' this spot.

SECOND BANANA. Wanna suck my dick now?

ADOLESCENT FEMALE. You're so strong!

SUBORDINATE FEMALE. Oh good God, by your own admission, you just beat up a retarded faggot. What exactly does that make you?

SECOND BANANA. A real man.

FIELD SCIENTIST. It makes the subordinate male the victor. He can maintain his status, which he has successfully defended today.

(*In the background, a clock begins to chime. After the first strike the characters begin to quickly don more clothing.*)

FIELD SCIENTIST. *(cont.)* Physical dominance is a powerful undercurrent that controls the lower classes; however, if we look at the evolution of a less physically driven society what do you think we will find? There will still be constant struggles for power, which will end in a victor and a poor defeated soul. Some will move up in society, others down, some will merely keep the status quo. Those who live past their time will undoubtedly fall. Time marches on.

(The clock strikes three times. The characters rush about frantically. All characters exit except for **ALPHA FEMALE**. **ALPHA FEMALE** *puts on an apron and begins to vacuum as all the characters exit. She should appear to become more like June Cleaver or Harriet. The* **ALPHA MALE**, **ADOLESCENT MALE, ADOLESCENT FEMALE, SECOND BANANA**, *and* **ALPHA FEMALE** *are something out of a 1950's sitcom.* **OUTSIDE FEMALE, OUTSIDE MALE**, *and* **SUBORDINATE FEMALE** *are more present-day. As each character enters, there should be canned applause, and the designer might consider the occasional, sparing use of a laugh track.)*

ALPHA FEMALE. Such a lovely, lovely floor. *(to vacuum)* You do your job so well you should get a medal. Oh my goodness, I think those cookies are almost done. Done, done, done.

(**SUBORDINATE FEMALE** *enters.)*

There's nothing like a clean house and the smell of fresh baking to fill one's soul. How could a woman be happier?

SUBORDINATE FEMALE. Mom, who are you talking to?

(**ADOLESCENT MALE** *enters and flops down with his book bag.* **FIELD SCIENTIST** *indicates* **ADOLESCENT MALE** *to* **JANE** *who "tags" him.)*

ALPHA FEMALE. Talking to, dear?

SUBORDINATE FEMALE. Yeah, I came in and you're talking to someone I presume.

ALPHA FEMALE. Why, to you, dear.

SUBORDINATE FEMALE. You didn't know I was here yet.

ALPHA FEMALE. Oh goodness! And you *are* here, back from finishing school.

SUBORDINATE FEMALE. College, Mom.

ALPHA FEMALE. Shhh. Not so loud, the neighbors might hear. Proper girls go to finishing school, not traipsing about to college. What does a woman need with college, unless she's there to find a nice college boy? That's it, isn't it? You've found a boy. I'm sure he's a lovely boy. Is he here?

SUBORDINATE FEMALE. You're getting a little Stepford on me here, Mom. Seriously, who were you talking to?

ALPHA FEMALE. You see it on television all the time now.

SUBORDINATE FEMALE. What's with all the 50s crap?

ALPHA FEMALE. Your father thinks we should get back to our "family values." Your father knows best. Now would you like a fresh-baked cookie? I made them special for you.

SUBORDINATE FEMALE. I don't like cookies. Does he make you dress like that?

ALPHA FEMALE. Nonsense, everyone loves cookies! Chocolate chip is your favorite isn't it? Everyone loves chocolate chip. *(begins to swoon)* I know it was my favorite when I was a little girl. *(drops to the floor)* Oooops. How did I get down here? I should get up. Very unsightly to be seen just lying around. *(She tries to get up and falls.)*

SUBORDINATE FEMALE. *(rushes to her)* Just stay there, Mom. Are you okay?

ALPHA FEMALE. Yes, just one of my spells. I'll be alright in a jiffy. Jiffy, jiffy, jiffy. Please don't tell your father. He'll get in one of his moods again.

ADOLESCENT MALE. *(rousing himself, but maintains a seated position)* Why?

ALPHA FEMALE. Goodness, when did you get home?

ADOLESCENT MALE. Uhhh, just now.

ALPHA FEMALE. Come here and give your mother a hug. Did you have a good day at school?

(**ALPHA FEMALE** *and* **ADOLESCENT MALE** *are still on the floor.*)

ADOLESCENT MALE. Tommy Tucker stole my milk money again.

SUBORDINATE FEMALE. *(to* **ALPHA FEMALE***)* How long has this been going on?

ALPHA FEMALE. About a week or so I guess.

ADOLESCENT MALE. Can I have a cookie?

SUBORDINATE FEMALE. Not, now Isaac. Mom's sick.

(**JANE** *is currently located on a stool, eating a cookie, watching as though it is a soap opera.* **FIELD SCIENTIST** *joins her, eating popcorn.* **JANE** *hands* **ADOLESCENT MALE** *a cookie. They sit as though entranced by television.*)

ALPHA FEMALE. Nonsense. I'm not sick at all. I'm not in the least bit sick. *(to* **ADOLESCENT MALE***)* We'll talk to your father when he gets home; he'll know exactly what to do. Your father says…

SUBORDINATE FEMALE. I don't give a flying fuck what father says…

ALPHA FEMALE. I will not have that kind of language in this house.

SUBORDINATE FEMALE. You're trying to change the subject.

ALPHA FEMALE. Of all the things a lady might say…

SUBORDINATE FEMALE. You should get this checked out. No one has to know.

ADOLESCENT MALE. I know.

SUBORDINATE FEMALE. Shut up.

ALPHA FEMALE. Don't speak to your brother that way. We can discuss this L-A-T-E-R.

SUBORDINATE FEMALE. Mom, he can spell. *(checking)* You can spell, can't you?

ADOLESCENT MALE. L-A-T-E-R.

ALPHA FEMALE. I've got to finish supper. Your uncle is coming over for dinner. Goodness! Is that the time? Your father will be home any minute.

SUBORDINATE FEMALE. Uncle Charlie's coming over? Does Dad know about this?

(**ADOLESCENT FEMALE** *enters to canned applause and wolf whistles. She smiles and waves at the audience.*)

ALPHA FEMALE. Where have you been, young lady?

ADOLESCENT FEMALE. Trying out for the school talent show.

ADOLESCENT MALE. Everyone one knows the only talent you have involves boys.

SUBORDINATE FEMALE. I thought Dad said Uncle Charlie couldn't come over here again.

ADOLESCENT MALE. He said over his dead body will that flaming goddamn fa...

ALPHA FEMALE. Young man, you will not use that language in this house.

ADOLESCENT MALE. But Dad's the one that said it.

ALPHA FEMALE. I will not tolerate it, regardless of who said it first. Remember, "family values."

ADOLESCENT MALE. Yes ma'am. Sorry, Mom. Can I have another cookie?

(**JANE** *gives* **ADOLESCENT MALE** *another cookie.*)

SUBORDINATE FEMALE. I hate to keep bringing this up, and all of you know I love Uncle Charlie, but...

ALPHA FEMALE. Now dear, is it true?

ADOLESCENT FEMALE. Is what true?

ALPHA FEMALE. About the boys?

ADOLESCENT MALE. Well on the boys bathroom it says that...

ADOLESCENT FEMALE. He's always trying to get me in trouble.

ADOLESCENT MALE. Am not.

ADOLESCENT FEMALE. Are too.

ADOLESCENT MALE. Am not.

ADOLESCENT FEMALE. Are too.

ADOLESCENT MALE. Am not.

ADOLESCENT FEMALE. Are too.

SUBORDINATE FEMALE. Enough.

ADOLESCENT MALE. She's been smooching with Tommy Tucker under the old oak tree behind the school.

ADOLESCENT FEMALE. You've been smooching with Tommy Tucker under the old oak tree behind the school.

ALPHA FEMALE. It sounds like soon we're going to have to have the birds and the bees talk.

SUBORDINATE FEMALE. They have MTV. You still have cable, right?

ALPHA FEMALE. Both of you put on something nice, your uncle is coming for dinner tonight.

ADOLESCENT MALE. Yea, Uncle Charlie.

ALPHA FEMALE. Upstairs, now.

ADOLESCENT FEMALE. But we don't have an upstairs.

ALPHA FEMALE. Don't you back talk me young lady. Now you march right upstairs and get changed, chop-chop.

(**ADOLESCENT MALE** *and* **ADOLESCENT FEMALE** *scurry off-stage.*)

Kind but firm. Remember, you must always be firm. That's the only way children will grow up properly. This is important to animals and children alike it is not so important what you say as the tone in which you say it.

SUBORDINATE FEMALE. Who are you talking to?

ALPHA FEMALE. What dear? Sorry it's so easy to get distracted sometimes. You understand don't you, dear?

SUBORDINATE FEMALE. Are you sure you're, okay?

ALPHA FEMALE. Fiddle-dee-dee. Your father says it's just in my head.

(**SECOND BANANA** *enters and he is somewhat effeminate.*)

SECOND BANANA. Hello, hello, hello! Anybody home?

SUBORDINATE FEMALE. Uncle Charlie, uhhh, are you into this family values thing too?

SECOND BANANA. Well, that's a fine how-do-you-do! You're growing up so fast. Just look at you.

ALPHA FEMALE. I thought you were bringing a friend.

SUBORDINATE FEMALE. A friend?

SECOND BANANA. He's going to meet me here.

SUBORDINATE FEMALE. A friend?

SECOND BANANA. You do know what kind of friend he is, don't you?

SUBORDINATE FEMALE. I have a pretty good idea.

SECOND BANANA. Is Jason here?

SUBORDINATE FEMALE. Did you hear the world explode, yet?

SECOND BANANA. I have got to go check my hair. I hate it when it won't cooperate. It's always acting up when I've got something important. My God, he'll be here any minute. I hope I've prepared him enough for this. Bringing them home to meet the family is such a big to do. Damn.

ALPHA FEMALE. Language.

SECOND BANANA. Does my brother know?

ALPHA FEMALE. Don't be silly.

SECOND BANANA. He does know I'm coming over?

ALPHA FEMALE. I know he would love to meet one of your friends.

SECOND BANANA. This is a *special* friend. You did tell Jason that I was going to be here tonight, didn't you?

ALPHA FEMALE. A special friend even better. I bet the two of you are quite close.

SUBORDINATE FEMALE. Dad will flip if he figures this out.

ALPHA FEMALE. Figures what out, dear?

SUBORDINATE FEMALE. About Uncle Charlie's "friend." Tell me you know what we're talking about.

ALPHA FEMALE. Of course I do, dear. Your uncle has invited his closest friend for dinner. Your father has been known to have special friends, too.

SUBORDINATE FEMALE. You're not listening to me, Mom.

ALPHA FEMALE. *(serious, not 50's at all)* You're not listening to me. Your father has a number of special friends that he invites to dinner from time to time to flaunt in my face. I am perfectly aware of the special nature of your uncle and the relationships he has with his friends, and I assure you, it's the same relationship your father has with his. *(back to 50's)* Silly me.

FIELD SCIENTIST. The vague references to a given universal knowledge in the household somehow make things more palatable. It makes it possible for the subordinate female and male to openly discuss taboo subjects with the alpha female, such as the subordinate male's sexual orientation, or her husband's constant philandering.

(**JANE** *shushes the* **FIELD SCIENTIST**.)

ALPHA FEMALE. I believe Mary will be joining us for dinner this evening.

SECOND BANANA. I'm really sorry, Elizabeth. I thought it was over with Jason and Mary. I always suspected something, but my brother and I don't really talk anymore. I'm sorry.

ALPHA FEMALE. You see why I had to invite you over. He's surprising me by bringing her home. I thought we could have our own surprise.

SECOND BANANA. This is a dangerous game you're playing. I don't mind helping you, of course. I'm sure Jason will just about stroke when he sees me, but...

ALPHA FEMALE. He won't act out in certain company.

SUBORDINATE FEMALE. This is a big gamble, Mom. You never know what Dad will do.

SECOND BANANA. Does she know?

SUBORDINATE FEMALE. She who?

ALPHA FEMALE. I know, I know I should tell her. It's just hard, I don't know if she could handle it.

SECOND BANANA. I could tell her, that would make Jason really happy. Nothing like opening the closet to find the family skeletons.

ALPHA FEMALE. I should really tell her.

SECOND BANANA. She should really hear it from her father.

SUBORDINATE FEMALE. I don't know if you've noticed this or not, but I'm right here.

ALPHA FEMALE. Of course we have, dear.

SUBORDINATE FEMALE. Mom, I think you owe me an explanation.

ALPHA FEMALE. I quite agree.

SUBORDINATE FEMALE. Well.

ALPHA FEMALE. Later dear, we have company.

SUBORDINATE FEMALE. When later?

ALPHA FEMALE. *(sing-song)* Later. By the way, Charlie, I hope your friend is everything you say he is.

(**OUTSIDE MALE** *enters. He is very effeminate.*)

OUTSIDE MALE. *(very quick)* This neighborhood is absolutely unbelievable. Every yard perfectly manicured. I feel like I'm in Oz. Just click my heels three times and ooop there's a topiary. Tell me is there property available in this area. It's simply fabulous. You never told me he lives in heaven you big lug. Oh my God, I left the bundt cake in the car I'll be right back. *(exiting)* I mean this is just fabulous.

SUBORDINATE FEMALE. Wow.

SECOND BANANA. Isn't he just adorable?

SUBORDINATE FEMALE. I'm not really sure…

ALPHA FEMALE. Enough of this sourpuss attitude! Why don't we sing some lovely carols?

SUBORDINATE FEMALE. Mom, it's July.

ALPHA FEMALE. Surely there's some lovely summer carols we could sing. You can try for mommy can't you?

FIELD SCIENTIST. Guilt can be a great controller. Females, not as physically strong as their male counterparts, had to learn ways to coerce others into obeying them. Unlike the alpha male's tendency to rule by power, the alpha female has had to learn to manipulate her surroundings and those around her to maintain her control. It is a time-honored tradition passed down from mother to daughter.

(Offstage, we hear the jingling of keys.)

ALPHA MALE. *(offstage)* I'm sure that this will be a big surprise.

OUTSIDE FEMALE. *(offstage)* I'm a little nervous.

SUBORDINATE FEMALE. Shit, they're here.

ALPHA FEMALE. Language.

SECOND BANANA. Maybe I should hide. Maybe this wasn't such a good idea. I could just slip out the back.

SUBORDINATE FEMALE. I think it's too late for that.

ALPHA FEMALE. I should really check on that roast. I'll be back in a jiffy. Jiffy, jiffy, jiffy.

SUBORDINATE FEMALE. Oh no you don't. You have to stay here with us.

(Keys jingle again.)

ALPHA MALE. *(offstage)* I can't wait to see the look on her face. Damn key.

ALPHA FEMALE. Everyone try to act normal. It might take him time to notice.

SUBORDINATE FEMALE. What he has to adjust to the light?

(The jingling ends and there is the opening of the lock. The lights fade except for the backlight behind the door.)

ALPHA MALE. Hi honey, I'm home.

(blackout)

ACT II

(The scene picks up right where Act I left off.)

ALPHA MALE. Hi honey, I'm home. *(applause)* I hope you don't mind I invited an old friend for dinner. *(To* **SECOND BANANA***)* What the hell are you doing here? *(He looks to the* **OUTSIDE FEMALE,** *then to the* **ALPHA FEMALE,** *then back to his brother.)* I mean, brother, it's so good to see you! It's been so long.

*(***ADOLESCENT MALE** *and* **ADOLESCENT FEMALE** *enter.)*

ADOLESCENT MALE. Daddy! Daddy, you're home!

ALPHA MALE. Why, yes I am! How's my big man? Look what I brought for you, my big man. *(pulls out football)* Are you ready? Catch.

*(***ADOLESCENT MALE** *ducks and screams like a girl.* **JANE** *catches the ball.)*

Oh good God.

ALPHA FEMALE. Language, dear.

ALPHA MALE. But the boy…

ALPHA FEMALE. Language.

ADOLESCENT FEMALE. Daddy, can I get you your slippers?

ALPHA MALE. Of course you can, dear. You've turned into quite a blossoming flower. Hasn't she Mary?

ADOLESCENT MALE. Girls are icky.

SECOND BANANA. I quite agree.

ALPHA MALE. *(ignoring* **SECOND BANANA***)* Now then, son, there was a time when I would agree with you, but you're coming to an age now when girls may look different to you than they did before.

ADOLESCENT MALE. Uncle Charlie thinks girls are icky.

ALPHA MALE. That is not appropriate conversation for the moment. *(to* **OUTSIDE FEMALE***)* I'm sorry, I'm being terribly rude.

OUTSIDE FEMALE. It's quite alright. It's just so different seeing your family around you. It's been so long.

SUBORDINATE FEMALE. It must put a new perspective on things.

ALPHA FEMALE. *(sing-song)* No helping.

OUTSIDE FEMALE. Is this Kate, my little Kate? I haven't seen you in so long. You've turned into quite the beautiful young woman. *(almost weeping)* Your mother must be so proud. Silly me to go on this way. It's just been so long since I've seen you. What ever have you been doing with yourself?

SUBORDINATE FEMALE. I could ask the same of you.

ALPHA FEMALE. *(entering)* She's been away at finishing school.

SUBORDINATE FEMALE. College, mom.

OUTSIDE FEMALE. I see.

ALPHA MALE. Yes, she's been studying—what have you been studying again, dear?

SUBORDINATE FEMALE. Bio-chem. But I plan to study law.

ALPHA MALE. No M-R-S degree for our little Katie.

SUBORDINATE FEMALE. I prefer to be called Kate, and have since I was five.

ALPHA MALE. Precious child, isn't she. Now my Little Jessie here just had the most beautiful dance recital. And our Isaac… *(struggling for anything to say)* can't say too much about him, now can we?

OUTSIDE FEMALE. So what are you up to, young man?

ADOLESCENT MALE. Bugs.

OUTSIDE FEMALE. I beg your pardon?

ADOLESCENT MALE. Bugs. I like bugs. I study bugs. I wish I were a bug, then somebody could just squash me and get it over with.

ALPHA MALE. What a kidder this one is. Son, really.

ALPHA FEMALE. He's going to grow up to be a—what was the word? You told me just the other day, dear…Oh yes, entomologist. Isn't that right, son?

ADOLESCENT MALE. I like bugs a lot.

FIELD SCIENTIST. As is true with some leaders, the alpha male is only dimly aware of the individual lives of his pack. The alpha male does have a soft spot for the adolescent female, only because it is easier to love those who love you unconditionally.

OUTSIDE MALE. *(offstage loudly and effeminate)* Oh my. Just simply fabulous.

SECOND BANANA. I think that's my friend. Excuse me, I should really go get him.

APLHA MALE. Friend?

ALPHA FEMALE. Just slipped my mind. I wanted to tell you Charlie and his friend are coming over for dinner.

ADOLESCENT MALE. Holy crap.

ALPHA FEMALE. Language, dear.

ALPHA MALE. Charlie's friend?

ALPHA FEMALE. Dear me, I hope there's enough room for everyone.

ALPHA MALE. My brother's "friend"?

ALPHA FEMALE. Yes, dear.

ALPHA MALE. What kind of friend is he?

ALPHA FEMALE. He didn't say. But you know, he's always been kind of a loner, I thought it would do him good to bring a friend. I told him to invite him.

ALPHA MALE. You did what? But you've never met this friend of his.

ALPHA FEMALE. Well, dear, it seemed like the Christian thing to do.

ALPHA MALE. I'm sure. But if you've never met him, he could be dangerous or a psychopath or something.

ALPHA FEMALE. I said he was your brother's friend, dear. I'm sure your brother wouldn't have dangerous friends, now, wouldn't you agree?

SUBORDINATE FEMALE. It's nice that Uncle Charlie is starting to make friends that are more like him, don't you think, Dad?

ALPHA FEMALE. No helping.

ALPHA MALE. What do you mean, more like him?

(*SECOND BANANA enters.*)

SECOND BANANA. He'll be here in just a second. Mary, it's been a while! So good to see you again!

ALPHA MALE. This friend of yours…what's he like?

FIELD SCIENTIST. The tactical changes in this class are truly fascinating. Let's watch as the subordinate male subverts the question. This is really where he comes into his own.

SECOND BANANA. Sorry, it's just been so long since I've seen Mary. You and my brother used to be so close. He must keep you hidden away nowadays. Are you still close?

OUTSIDE FEMALE. I suppose you could say we're still close…

SUBORDINATE FEMALE. Quite close?

ALPHA FEMALE. (*sing-song*) No helping.

FIELD SCIENTIST. Of course many people in this class are good at tactical changes.

OUTSIDE FEMALE. My, it is rather warm in here. Would one of you be kind enough to get me a glass of water?

ADOLESCENT MALE. A cup.

OUTSIDE FEMALE. Excuse me?

ADOLESCENT MALE. A cup of water. We're not allowed to take the glasses outside the kitchen except at meal times.

OUTSIDE FEMALE. Isn't that interesting?

ALPHA FEMALE. (*to ADOLESCENT FEMALE*) Would you be kind enough to get Mrs…?

OUTSIDE FEMALE. Miss. I've never been married. You know that, Elizabeth.

ALPHA FEMALE. Yes, how silly of me. How easy it is to forget who's married and who isn't? Would you agree, Mary? Would you be kind enough to get Mary a cup of water from the kitchen? Thank you, dear.

(ADOLESCENT FEMALE *exits. There is a pause in the action while everyone looks around uncomfortably.* OUTSIDE MALE *enters and he is now flamboyantly gay.*)

OUTSIDE MALE. What a place you have here, sir. I mean, the window treatment is fabulous! Be honest, did you decorate it yourself or did you have a professional do it?

ADOLESCENT MALE. A professional, what?

OUTSIDE MALE. What a cute boy. Just a question I would have asked at your age.

ALPHA MALE. What is that supposed to mean?

ADOLESCENT MALE. Are you my uncle's friend?

ALPHA FEMALE. Chop-chop dear. Why don't you go help your sister?

ADOLESCENT MALE. Why does nobody ever answer my questions?

OUTSIDE MALE. Well, yes we are friends.

ALPHA FEMALE. Upstairs.

ADOLESCENT MALE. But there isn't one...

ALPHA MALE. Don't back talk your mother. Now.

ADOLESCENT MALE. But I looked everywhere last time and...

SUBORDINATE FEMALE. Just go.

(ADOLESCENT MALE *exits.*)

OUTSIDE MALE. Well, I'm Austin, and you must be Lizzy. A rapture of beauty just like Charlie said you were.

ALPHA FEMALE. He said that about me? What a charmer!

SUBORDINATE FEMALE. Wow. You're so not what I expected.

OUTSIDE MALE. And you must be Kate. Bio-chem major, right?

SUBORDINATE FEMALE. Yeah.

(**ADOLESCENT MALE** *enters with water.*)

ALPHA MALE. *(to* **ALPHA FEMALE** *under his breath)* He's browner than I thought he would be.

ALPHA FEMALE. Please don't, dear.

ALPHA MALE. I'm afraid I'm going to have to ask your friend to leave. There just isn't enough to go around.

ALPHA FEMALE. Nonsense, dear. I've made plenty for everybody, and for whatever's left over, I bought Tupperware containers. *(to audience)* Tupperware is the greatest invention a woman could ever ask for. Anything that makes a woman a better wife and mother is an invention of great note. Pretty exciting stuff, huh?

ALPHA MALE. It's the table I'm worried about. There simply isn't enough room.

ALPHA FEMALE. Sure there is. We can all squeeze together. I added a leaf to the table, and borrowed some nice folding chairs from the neighbors.

ALPHA MALE. The neighbors. Do the neighbors know about this? Are you trying to humiliate me? What are people going to think? People have lost their jobs for less, and you bring this into our household? Do you know what you've done?

(**ALPHA MALE** *goes to backhand* **ALPHA FEMALE** *and freezes.* **ADOLESCENT FEMALE** *enters. Lights begin to flash and music for game show begins. Everyone suddenly looks excited.*)

FIELD SCIENTIST. There is only one thing the middle class strives to more than their nineteen fifties role models, and that is to win a game show.

ADOLESCENT FEMALE. I love games, just ask anyone.

(**FIELD SCIENTIST** *takes on the persona of a game show host.* **JANE** *unhappily takes on the role of a "Vanna White" type character.*)

FIELD SCIENTIST. Of course you do. Who wants to play?

ADOLESCENT FEMALE. Can I win a prize?

FIELD SCIENTIST. You already have.

ADOLESCENT FEMALE. Really?

FIELD SCIENTIST. It's called an STD.

ADOLESCENT FEMALE. I won! I won! I've never gotten anything before!

FIELD SCIENTIST. This is one prize that could last a lifetime.

ADOLESCENT MALE. What kind of game is it?

FIELD SCIENTIST. It's called Middle Class Morality.

ALPHA MALE. Sounds suitable for children.

FIELD SCIENTIST. It's suitable for everybody. This is the way it works, whoever gets to a hundred points first wins a fabulous prize.

ADOLESCENT FEMALE. You mean I can win again?

FIELD SCIENTIST. Once you're a winner you can really never stop winning, now, can you? Let's introduce our contestants. First, the breadwinner, the head-honcho of the family, let's hear it for the man.

(canned applause)

Now here's the thing, the alpha male has to keep himself as the strongest of the bunch, but being a modern man, he wants to be seen as sensitive.

ALPHA MALE. That's right, I care about my fellow man. Jesus cared for everyone, and we should follow his example.

FIELD SCIENTIST. But not so sensitive that he loses his masculinity.

ALPHA MALE. Women shouldn't have to work. They were born to be mothers. Women need to stay home and take care of the family and children. I'm just here to provide for them, keep them in line if necessary. Where would any of them be without me?

(applause)

FIELD SCIENTIST. The middle class teaches tolerance. Let's look at the alpha female. What is it that separates you from other people, lesser people, if you will?

ALPHA FEMALE. Well, there are certain words and phrases we simply do not use.

ALPHA MALE. You can't say nigger, jig-a-boo, or darkie.

FIELD SCIENTIST. Let's let her answer on her own. It's your turn, dear.

ALPHA FEMALE. Well, I grew up calling them jungle bunnies, but not anymore.

ALPHA MALE. You'd think you could, but you can't. Unless, of course, you're out with the boys swapping jokes for the night. Hell, we can't even call them negro anymore. They want to be called colored.

FIELD SCIENTIST. This isn't your turn.

ALPHA MALE. Why the hell can't we just call them all brown? That's all anyone is who isn't white, right?

OUTSIDE MALE. Technically, you're not white, you're actually more of a peachy color.

FIELD SCIENTIST. The middle class teaches tolerance—Ten points to the alpha male for keeping those undesirables at arm's length.

ALPHA MALE. Yeah, ten points!

(applause)

FIELD SCIENTIST. *(to* **ADOLESCENT FEMALE***)* This one's for you.

(wolf whistle sound effect)

What would you like to do if you could do anything?

ADOLESCENT FEMALE. Of course I would like to end world hunger, and I am so ready for that question if I break the top ten on Miss America.

FIELD SCIENTIST. But what do you really think?

ADOLESCENT FEMALE. We can give to the Christian Children's Fund and feel better about ourselves. I mean no one would actually want to go touch one of those icky babies, would they? I mean, yuck.

FIELD SCIENTIST. Ten points for yucky babies and general duplicity.

ADOLESCENT FEMALE. *(sing-song to her brother)* Whoo-hoo. I got ten points for yucky babies and you don't have anything because you suck.

ADOLESCENT MALE. Do not.

ADOLESCENT FEMALE. You smell.

ADOLESCENT MALE. You smell.

FIELD SCIENTIST. The middle class must strive to hide their true nature. What's the best way to hide?

SECOND BANANA. In the closet. I can act straight if I have to. I can even talk about football.

OUTSIDE MALE. I love a good tight end.

FIELD SCIENTIST. This is to the subordinate male.

SECOND BANANA. I can hide it if I have to. I'm good at it. I've been practicing acting like a real boy my whole life. It's not like I'm going to get killed for it, right?

FIELD SCIENTIST. Ten points for hiding. *(to* **OUTSIDE MALE***)* How do you feel about hiding?

OUTSIDE MALE. I don't know. Being a—what'd you call us?—"brown" fairy certainly isn't helpful. Being a pretty white boy helps a lot. If I were white, I'm sure it would be a lot different.

FIELD SCIENTIST. But a leopard can't change its spots, now, can it? Sorry, you lose ten points.

OUTSIDE MALE. For what?

FIELD SCIENTIST. Only white people do well at game shows, you know that.

OUTSIDE MALE. I lose ten points for being brown?

FIELD SCIENTIST. You're absolutely right. I gotta give you your ten points back for that. You're back up to zero. *(to* **OUTSIDE FEMALE***)* And what's your place in this society?

OUTSIDE FEMALE. It's probably about par for being the "other woman," and that's just what they say to your face. Do you think I wanted to end up forty, never been married, and having an affair with a married man? Do you think this is what my parents wanted me to be when I grew up? As long as I'm quiet and smile, people will keep their talk behind closed doors. That's the best I can hope for.

FIELD SCIENTIST. Too much drama, this is a game show, not a talk show. I've gotta take ten points for your response and ten more for your lack of Caucasian background.

OUTSIDE FEMALE. I'm half white.

ALPHA MALE. She should just lose five for that.

FIELD SCIENTIST. For your sense of fair play, you get eighty points.

SUBORDINATE FEMALE. He's just saying that because he's banging her.

FIELD SCIENTIST. Minus five for speaking out of turn.

SUBORDINATE FEMALE. But…

FIELD SCIENTIST. You want to make it ten?

SUBORDINATE FEMALE. This isn't fair.

FIELD SCIENTIST. Crying the unfair card is worth ten points in your favor. The unfair is a great attribute of the middle class.

SUBORDINATE FEMALE. This game is rigged.

FIELD SCIENTIST. Of course it is.

ALPHA FEMALE. We must strive to never deviate from the norm, and do our best to keep up with the Joneses.

ADOLESCENT MALE. Yeah, if I won the lottery I'd have it made. I could make people like me.

FIELD SCIENTIST. Ten points for views that money cures all ills. Good job, boy.

ADOLESCENT MALE. Really?

FIELD SCIENTIST. No, not really, you lose twenty for acting with no self-confidence. Not manly enough.

ALPHA MALE. Damn it! Keep your mouth shut! Take away another ten for embarrassing me.

FIELD SCIENTIST. Tell you what I'll do, I'll take away twenty.

ADOLESCENT MALE. But Dad…

ALPHA FEMALE. Not now, dear.

SUBORDINATE FEMALE. This is bullshit.

FIELD SCIENTIST. Of course, no matter how much you strive to break the barriers, if the middle class raises you, you will always have their mores.

ADOLESCENT MALE. What's a mores?

SUBORDINATE FEMALE. I am not like them.

FIELD SCIENTIST. Denial is worth ten points.

SUBORDINATE FEMALE. I want to see a world where everyone is equal.

ALPHA MALE. That's called communism and we know it doesn't work.

OUTSIDE MALE. Why can't we have gay marriages?

ALPHA MALE. That is not what God intended. Marriage is between a man and a woman.

FIELD SCIENTIST. Three points for bringing up God.

OUTSIDE MALE. Cause straight people certainly haven't fucked marriage up.

ALPHA FEMALE. Language. In many ways, it doesn't matter what you say, but in the tone in which you say it.

ALPHA MALE. Why don't we let people just marry a box turtle?

FIELD SCIENTIST. Ahhh, the sanctity of marriage! What a great question! How do we feel about that?

ALPHA MALE. God's laws should not be broken. He alone showed us the way. He speaks to us in Matthew...

ALPHA FEMALE. And what about the Ten Commandments? Doesn't that speak to fidelity?

ALPHA MALE. She is not another man's wife. And besides, if I've told you once I've told you a thousand times, if you took better care of yourself, this would never have happened. A man has needs, if his wife does not fulfill them, you can't blame him for his actions.

ALPHA FEMALE. Perhaps I could lose a few pounds, but I could never lose ten years.

ALPHA MALE. We should be grateful that we live in the freest country in the world.

FIELD SCIENTIST. One point awarded for waving the flag. Final question. This one's up for grabs. Who is the most important person in the family and why?

ALPHA MALE. Me, because I'm the man.

FIELD SCIENTIST. I'm going to have to ask you to expand on that.

ALPHA MALE. I'm the white, heterosexual man that this country was founded on and led by. You can do anything in this country as long as you're free, white, and twenty-one.

FIELD SCIENTIST. That's right.

(canned applause)

ALPHA MALE. What do I win?

FIELD SCIENTIST. All the positions the world can offer a white man. You can win anything and be anyone.

OUTSIDE FEMALE. What about the rest of us?

FIELD SCIENTIST. You can have Oprah.

SUBORDINATE FEMALE. This is bullshit.

FIELD SCIENTIST. It certainly is.

ADOLESCENT MALE. I don't like this game anymore.

FIELD SCIENTIST. Then you don't have to play. Why don't we pick up where we left off? You know what you have to do now, don't you? You *are* the man.

ALPHA MALE. I *am* the man.

(Scene returns to normal, and actors resume their previous positions.)

I'm afraid your friend will have to go.

ALPHA FEMALE. I'm sorry.

ALPHA MALE. I will not be made a laughing stock.

SUBORDINATE FEMALE. I think you have done plenty of that yourself.

FIELD SCIENTIST. When a lower ranking female questions the divine authority of the alpha male, the results are never pretty.

ALPHA MALE. *(grabs her, shaking her)* What exactly are you trying to imply, young lady? You are not so big that I can't take you across my knee and spank you.

OUTSIDE FEMALE. Take your hands off her. I knew I should have kept her with me.

ALPHA MALE. *(to* **OUTSIDE FEMALE,** *still holding* **SUBORDINATE FEMALE***)* This isn't about you. You stay out of this.

OUTSIDE FEMALE. Leave her alone.

SUBORDINATE FEMALE. Why would you care anyway? You're the problem.

OUTSIDE FEMALE. You don't understand.

SUBORDINATE FEMALE. I think I understand plenty, as far as your concerned.

OUTSIDE FEMALE. You don't know the whole story. I am so sorry, I always wanted to tell you, but everyone wanted what was in your best interest.

ALPHA FEMALE. We didn't want you to get your feelings hurt, dear.

ALPHA MALE. It's time you left.

ALPHA FEMALE. Who's leaving, dear?

ALPHA MALE. *(indicating* **SECOND BANANA** *and* **OUTSIDE MALE***)* Both of them.

SECOND BANANA. I beg your pardon?

ALPHA MALE. You heard me. God, I should have taken care of this years ago.

OUTSIDE FEMALE. Didn't you ever wonder who your birth-mother was?

ALPHA MALE. This is not the time to deal with this, Mary.

SUBORDINATE FEMALE. I don't understand.

ALPHA FEMALE. You should tell her. It's time.

OUTSIDE FEMALE. I can't.

ALPHA FEMALE. We decided together what was best for her…

ALPHA MALE. And that was to keep silent. We swore an oath.

SECOND BANANA. If that's what you call it.

ALPHA MALE. You will leave this house this instant. You are not welcome here, not will you ever be welcome again.

SECOND BANANA. But we're blood. You remember blood, don't you brother.

ALPHA MALE. Company or no company, you will leave this house immediately. Or else.

SECOND BANANA. Or else, what?

ALPHA MALE. Try me and you'll find out.

SECOND BANANA. Oh, for Chrissakes. *(to* **SUBORDINATE FEMALE***)* Mary is your mother.

SUBORDINATE FEMALE. What?

OUTSIDE MALE. No.

SECOND BANANA. Sorry, it just sort of slipped out.

ALPHA MALE. How dare you!

SECOND BANANA. You know how these little slips can happen, don't you Jason.

OUTSIDE FEMALE. I always wanted to tell you, but I didn't think it was my place.

SUBORDINATE FEMALE. Exactly whose place did you think it was?

SECOND BANANA. On the upshot, he's really your father, if you want to think of it as an upshot.

ALPHA MALE. That's enough!

SECOND BANANA. Not really, there's more.

ALPHA MALE. *(speaking slowly and methodically)* Charlie, if you value your life, you'll hold your tongue.

*(**SECOND BANANA** nods, sits crossing his legs, and in a gossipy tone turns to the **SUBORDINATE FEMALE**.)*

SECOND BANANA. He knocked her up when your mom and dad first got married. Everyone thought it would be better if he and your mom raised you. They thought you'd have a better chance in society, and that way he didn't father a bastard, but a legitimate child. You even looked pretty white, everyone was so pleased.

ADOLESCENT FEMALE. Dad? Is it true?

SECOND BANANA. She was sixteen, and you were pushing thirty, and you question my morals?

SUBORDINATE FEMALE. You slept with her when she was sixteen?

ADOLESCENT FEMALE. I'm sixteen.

ADOLESCENT MALE. You never slept with Dad, did you?

SUBORDINATE FEMALE. You slimy, fucking bastard.

ADOLESCENT MALE. Does this mean I have to sleep with Dad?

ALPHA MALE. You swore you'd never tell. We all swore.

SECOND BANANA. Well I guess I unswore it then.

FIELD SCIENTIST. The alpha male is really losing ground here. He's going to have to recover his authority or risk losing it forever. He's going to have to attack the subordinate male in a way that the others will not argue.

ALPHA MALE. It's your immoral ways that brought you to this. I should have done to you a long time ago, what our father did to me. He beat it out of me. He showed me the way.

(**SECOND BANANA** *throws down the penalty flag.* **JANE** *blows a whistle and waves her arms that the play is now over.* **JANE** *picks up the penalty.* **ALPHA MALE** *is agitated and starts miming kicking dirt on her shoes.* **SECOND BANANA** *begins to plead his case and* **ALPHA MALE** *exits.*)

FIELD SCIENTIST. As anger builds, the social constructs of the middle class crumble. One by one, man begins to show his truest nature. Not the divine nature, but the animalistic one. The alpha male is being challenged on many sides. No doubt there is only one way he feels he can prove his dominance.

(*There is a gunshot offstage. All the characters freeze and slowly turn to the source of the sound.* **ALPHA MALE** *enters carrying a rifle and appearing aggressive. All characters sans the* **FIELD SCIENTIST** *scamper off stage.*)

ALPHA MALE. Pull.

(*A clock ticking is heard. The chime strikes three times.* **ALPHA MALE** *tracks the target and fires again. The* **ALPHA MALE** *is at a downstage corner of the stage while the other characters reset the stage to the upper class. The* *study is an expensive one. The room does not need a full setting but a few nice wingback chairs to imply the wealth of the household. The* **OUTSIDE FEMALE** *enters and cleans away the coffee cup. All characters in this scene are wearing more clothes and more clothing layers than in previous scenes.* **FIELD SCIENTIST** *ducks as the last shot is fired, and his Safari Hat has returned.)*

FIELD SCIENTIST. We catch up with our group, who have now made their home in this lovely clearing. As you can see, the fields are lush, hunting is plentiful, and water is easily accessed. This group enjoys more leisure time than most. They receive only the finest. The soft afternoon sun warms the chill away. Occasionally, we can find one of them sunning themselves in the late afternoon by the pond, after a hard day of leisure activity. Imagine, if you will, the amount a society could improve itself if given enough leisure time.

ALPHA MALE. Pull.

(ALPHA MALE *fires shot again, then crosses into the study.* **ALPHA MALE** *makes himself a drink and grabs the* **OUTSIDE FEMALE,** *who jumps in surprise.)*

ALPHA FEMALE. I see you haven't lost your touch with the help.

(ALPHA MALE *laughs.)*

FIELD SCIENTIST. Because of their sedentary lifestyle, they do not always hold onto their communication skills, for they do not rely on them to survive as heavily as most.

(ALPHA MALE *grunts at* **OUTSIDE FEMALE,** *who was trying to avoid him, and she exits quickly.)*

FIELD SCIENTIST. In a different setting, the alpha male might have to communicate with his whole clan to organize a hunt, to bring down big game. But as you can see here, there is little communication between the clan units. There is little need.

ALPHA FEMALE. Must you make such a racket with that

thing? I should be resting, you know.

(**ALPHA MALE** *grunts.*)

Is that your attempt at an apology?

(**ALPHA MALE** *laughs.*)

Rest, they tell me rest. Remission is a fabulous thing, isn't it? When you're dying, they want you to fight. When you're well, they want you to rest.

OUTSIDE FEMALE. *(entering)* Everything is ready for our guests.

ALPHA FEMALE. Thank you, dear.

(**OUTSIDE FEMALE** *curtsies and exits.*)

ALPHA MALE. What guests? I don't remember us discussing any guests.

ALPHA FEMALE. That's because we didn't discuss it, dear.

ALPHA MALE. Oh God, did you invite more of your riff-raff friends for some cause you are working on?   What are we—saving whales this week? The African Tree Frog? How about cancer research, or is that too self-serving?

ALPHA FEMALE. Perhaps you should try going to yours.

ALPHA MALE. A little work wouldn't hurt you, you know. Maybe help you drop a little of that baggage.

ALPHA FEMALE. Yes, the baggage.

FIELD SCIENTIST. In this case, the bickering in no way denigrates the alpha male. He would have to be listening to the comments from the alpha female in order for her to elicit an emotional response from him.

ALPHA FEMALE. I should go prepare for our guests.

ALPHA MALE. *(making himself another drink)* Perhaps you could lacquer on a few more layers of makeup while you're at it, might help hide those looks of yours.

FIELD SCIENTIST. The alpha male is good at this game. He knows his would-be adversary well. If he can keep her off balance, he can keep her at bay. Of course, some would find it silly to believe that a mere female could match wits against a higher ranked male to begin with.

ALPHA FEMALE. You know what made me fall in love with you? Your compassion.

ALPHA MALE. You know what made me fall in love with you? Your money.

ALPHA FEMALE. Does it irritate you that I survived?

ALPHA MALE. Who's coming over?

ALPHA FEMALE. It's a surprise.

ALPHA MALE. I don't like surprises. Every time there's been a surprise from you, it's been to let me know that we have another useless offspring on the way.

ALPHA FEMALE. I suppose I have received similar surprises from you.

ALPHA MALE. What's-her-name didn't turn out so bad, now, did she?

ALPHA FEMALE. Kate is her name, and no she did not. I'm surprised you have some decent recessive genes.

ALPHA MALE. Hell of a lot better than the ones you've turned out.

ALPHA FEMALE. That would be your dominant genes.

ALPHA MALE. I personally always place the blame on the bitch. You're the one that whelped them.

OUTSIDE FEMALE. (*entering*) The first guests are arriving.

ALPHA FEMALE. Thank you, Mary. Do show them up after they get their things squared away.

ALPHA MALE. I did not give my consent to houseguests.

ALPHA FEMALE. No, you did not. I did.

ALPHA MALE. (*to* **OUTSIDE FEMALE**) They will not be staying.

ALPHA FEMALE. (*to* **ALPHA MALE**) Dearest, let's not have a scene. (*to* **OUTSIDE FEMALE**) Please show our guests up. Thank you very much, Mary.

FIELD SCIENTIST. The alpha female has really laid the groundwork here on this one. There is no doubt she has been planning this particular attack for months.

ALPHA FEMALE. Do you know what today is? It's our wedding anniversary. Funny, I thought it would have been etched in your memory. I believe it was twenty-five years ago today I walked in on you *in flagrante delicto* with the maid.

ALPHA MALE. *(making himself a drink)* This is not significant, nor is it new.

ALPHA FEMALE. We did get a beautiful child out of your affair. Mary signed her away to us. Everyone was duly impressed that you would adopt a child so early in your marriage.

ALPHA MALE. It sounded quite good didn't it? I was rather proud of that one.

FIELD SCIENTIST. The alpha male is really showing his control here. The alpha female is just allowing him to feel safe. Lulling him into a false sense of security. Given her weakened physical condition, it could be a good tactic. The females of this species must turn to alternate tactics to compensate for their physical weaknesses and lesser mental states.

(JANE clicks her clipboard.)

ALPHA MALE. Who is coming to celebrate this, what do you call it, anniversary?

ALPHA FEMALE. Why, our wonderful offspring have come to recognize and celebrate our auspicious beginnings some twenty-five years ago.

ALPHA MALE. Lovely. Enjoy this while you can my dear. It is your anniversary as well. However, for this little stunt, which I am willing to play along with to save face, there will be a price.

ALPHA FEMALE. I'm certain I've gotten a taste over the years, of you at your worst. But I've never truly allowed you to see me at my worst.

ALPHA MALE. How exciting. Is this a challenge?

(ADOLESCENT FEMALE and ADOLESCENT MALE enter.)

FIELD SCIENTIST. As the offspring enter, one wonders what their place will be in society outside of their family unit. Can the adolescent male grow to become an alpha male?

ADOLESCENT MALE. Can you smell that? That was a good one, and that was all me.

ADOLESCENT FEMALE. Mother, control him.

ALPHA FEMALE. Your genes at work.

ADOLESCENT MALE. What?

ALPHA FEMALE. Come here and give your mother a hug.

ADOLESCENT FEMALE. You squeeze too tight.

ALPHA FEMALE. You're just too skinny, that's why it feels so tight. It's just so good to see you. I could eat you up and never let you go.

ADOLESCENT MALE. We're reading about cannibalism in school. *Lord of the Flies*. I really like Piggy.

ALPHA MALE. That's great, son. It's nice to know you're… um, reading now. Give your dad a firm handshake. You call that firm? Let me show you firm.

(**ADOLESCENT MALE** *squeals in pain.*)

For Chrissakes, son, you're going to have to act like a man sometime.

ALPHA FEMALE. Let him be.

ALPHA MALE. All your mothering him. That's what's done it to him.

ALPHA FEMALE. He's just a sensitive, artistic-type.

ALPHA MALE. I've never seen any artist tendencies.

ADOLESCENT FEMALE. Hello! I came here to see the two of you. You could at least pretend you notice me.

ALPHA MALE. How's my prettiest girl? We don't mean to ignore you pumpkin. Who's the prettiest girl in the world?

ADOLESCENT FEMALE. Me. Which is why I don't get it. You always pay more attention to him. You're always talking about him, like he's more interesting or something. You don't even seem to care what lines I'm wearing this fall.

ALPHA MALE. Well, pumpkin, I've been very busy at work, you know how it goes, and with your mother's recovery, which I thank God for every day, I've just been more wrapped up in my own affairs than usual.

ALPHA FEMALE. You could always turn a phrase.

(SECOND BANANA enters.)

SECOND BANANA. Is that what they're calling it now?

ADOLESCENT MALE. Uncle Charlie! Uncle Charlie!

ADOLESCENT FEMALE. Wow! I didn't know you were going to be here. Mom, why didn't you tell us?

ALPHA FEMALE. I've got lots of surprises in store for tonight.

SECOND BANANA. For my favorite nephew: Godiva chocolate. I know it's your favorite.

ADOLESCENT MALE. Gimme, gimme, gimme.

ALPHA FEMALE. You know he's on a restrictive diet.

SECOND BANANA. True, but how often does he get to see his favorite uncle?

ALPHA MALE. Bribing them with candy, now, are you? That seems typical, from what I've heard about your type. Get them while they're young.

SECOND BANANA. I learned from the best.

ALPHA MALE. If you value your job I suggest you nod and smile like a good boy.

ADOLESCENT FEMALE. This is what my therapist warned me about. I really don't know if I should even come home. She says it's mentally unhealthy for me. She says it's restrictive on my development.

SECOND BANANA. Perhaps this will help your development. For the lovely lady: diamonds are a girl's best friend.

ADOLESCENT FEMALE. I love it! Oh thank you so much Uncle Charlie! Diamonds go with everything you know. You are so thoughtful.

ALPHA MALE. *(making himself a drink)* Where's your lesser half?

SECOND BANANA. Parking the car, thank you for asking. You might want to lay off that stuff, Jason.

ALPHA MALE. Sure is taking him a while.

SECOND BANANA. I told him not to rush. He should take time to enjoy the grounds. I told him it was best not to bring any flowers in, they wilt as soon as they come inside.

ALPHA MALE. What's this one's name?

SECOND BANANA. Austin.

ALPHA MALE. Didn't we have a manservant by that name once?

ALPHA FEMALE. It's so hard for you to remember the men isn't it? *(to* **ADOLESCENT MALE***)* Silly me, how is school going this semester?

ADOLESCENT MALE. It sucks.

ADOLESCENT FEMALE. He always says that. I've had to listen to that all the way here. I mean, really, can't you book us separate flights or something?

ADOLESCENT MALE. You suck.

ALPHA FEMALE. Now honey, do we need to send you back to sensitivity classes?

ALPHA MALE. Sensitivity classes. You sent him to… is that what's wrong with him? Men aren't meant to be sensitive. I suppose I should feel lucky he came out of it without wearing a dress. There will be no further classes of this sort imposed on any son of mine at any time.

ADOLESCENT MALE. They sucked anyway.

ADOLESCENT FEMALE. See, it's always about him. How does he always demand the attention? I'm sure this is stunting my intellectual growth.

ADOLESCENT MALE. Like you know what that means.

ADOLESCENT FEMALE. Like you know what that means. Dad.

ALPHA MALE. Boy, leave your sister alone.

ADOLESCENT MALE. She started it.

ALPHA MALE. I don't pay for your damn boarding school so you can backtalk me. *(shaking him)* Your friends think it's okay to be disrespectful to your family? Well, do they?

ADOLESCENT MALE. *(quietly)* I don't have any friends.

ALPHA MALE. Louder.

ADOLESCENT MALE. I said, I don't have any friends.

ALPHA MALE. One more time.

ADOLESCENT MALE. *(whimpering)* I don't have any friends.

FIELD SCIENTIST. This particular alpha male has always enjoyed the humiliation factor.

SECOND BANANA. Jason, come on, that's enough.

ALPHA MALE. It's enough when I say it's enough. This boy needs a man's influence to turn out as something less than a total disaster. It's time I took controlling interest in my son. I can see what having had a soft hand on him has done to his natural dominance.

SECOND BANANA. Jason, really. Do we really need to hear your theories on survival of the fittest again? How some of us were born to lead? It's old. He's not you. He's not going to be you, no matter how much you want it.

ALPHA MALE. *(releasing the* **ADOLESCENT MALE***)* Don't you know your place in this family by now? The only reason decent people even deign to speak to you is because of me.

SECOND BANANA. Who do you think keeps the company solvent? We've showed profit every quarter since I was brought on.

*(***OUTSIDE MALE*** enters with gifts, jovial and unaware of the tension already in the room.)*

OUTSIDE MALE. Congratulations! Congratulations! Well hello, everyone! Twenty-five years is quite an accomplishment. Certainly gives us something to live up to here. Where shall I put all these gifts?

ALPHA FEMALE. Why don't you just set them over here?

OUTSIDE MALE. Got my camera ready for the pictures of the happy couple.

SECOND BANANA. Maybe this isn't such a good time for pictures.

OUTSIDE MALE. Oh.

ALPHA MALE. Why not?

ADOLESCENT MALE. It'll go with all the other pictures.

ALPHA FEMALE. Don't be such a sourpuss. We have the kids home for a whole weekend, don't we kids?

(**SUBORDINATE FEMALE** *enters with* **OUTSIDE FEMALE.**)

ADOLESCENT MALE. I… uh… gotta fly back tomorrow. I've got a chemistry final.

ADOLESCENT FEMALE. Me too. Chemistry.

SUBORDINATE FEMALE. But it's just October guys. If you're going to lie, you have to do better than that. You don't have finals in October.

ALPHA MALE. So glad you could make it.

SUBORDINATE FEMALE. Are you kidding? I wouldn't miss this for the world.

ALPHA MALE. I bet. It warms the cockles of my heart to have the whole family here for this monumental occasion.

SUBORDINATE FEMALE. Really? I didn't know you had a heart.

ADOLESCENT MALE. Or cockles.

ALPHA MALE. I suppose you took time out of your busy school schedule to come to your mother's special day.

SUBORDINATE FEMALE. I think it's more your special day, Dad.

ADOLESCENT FEMALE. Wouldn't it be about the same?

SUBORDINATE FEMALE. I think I've learned over the years, not all things are created equal.

ALPHA MALE. Then I have taught you well.

SUBORDINATE FEMALE. As far as school goes, I passed the Bar two years ago.

ALPHA MALE. A lawyer in the family, huh? That seems like a good job for you. Righting wrongs. That was always your specialty.

SUBORDINATE FEMALE. Still is.

ALPHA MALE. Spitting image of your mother.

SUBORDINATE FEMALE. *(to* **ALPHA MALE***)* You know, I'm a professional now. A professional woman, you can't treat me the way you used too. I've gone out and earned other people's respect, but with you...

ALPHA MALE. Please, what do you have to say to me, that you've kept bottled up all these years? *(pause)* I'm waiting. I'm sure you've been planning this speech for years, so let's hear it. *(pause)* That's what I thought. You're just as gutless as the rest.

SECOND BANANA. I object.

FIELD SCIENTIST. Overruled.

ADOLESCENT MALE. I second that objection, duh.

ADOLESCENT FEMALE. You can't second an objection.

FIELD SCIENTIST. *(producing a gavel)* Order in the court. Can I have order in the court?

(We should hear court music transition, i.e. People's Court *or* Law and Order, *something distinctive*. The characters all react to the sound as if to say, "Where did that come from?" with the exception of the* **ALPHA MALE, FIELD SCIENTIST***, and* **JANE***. Minimal changes are made to set up the courtroom appearance so that the* **ALPHA MALE** *is at the defense table and the* **FIELD SCIENTIST** *is the Judge.* **JANE** *is playing the part of the Stenographer.)*

I will read the next docket. The people versus the Alpha Male. What are the charges?

SUBORDINATE FEMALE. We charge my father with crimes against his clan, and we question his leadership as the Alpha Male.

FIELD SCIENTIST. Who is representing the defendant?

ALPHA MALE. I do not need any representation. I will represent myself.

FIELD SCIENTIST. Very well, how do you plead?

ALPHA MALE. Not guilty.

FIELD SCIENTIST. That sounds good enough to me. Let's take a recess.

SUBORDINATE FEMALE. Begging Your Honor's pardon, but I believe we are still allowed to make our case in this forum. Is it not the nature of this court to allow...

FIELD SCIENTIST. *(sighs)* Blah, blah, blah. If you must.

ALPHA MALE. Case, as if you have one.

FIELD SCIENTIST. You may call your first witness.

SUBORDINATE FEMALE. The people call the first-born male son of the alpha male, Isaac, to the stand.

ALPHA MALE. Please, what kind of witness can he make against me?

(**ADOLESCENT MALE** *moves to the witness stand.*)

ADOLESCENT MALE. What do I do?

SUBORDINATE FEMALE. Just answer the questions.

ALPHA MALE. Objection, she's coaching the witness.

FIELD SCIENTIST. Sustained.

ADOLESCENT FEMALE. How is that coaching the witness?

FIELD SCIENTIST. One more outburst and I will ask you to leave the courtroom.

SUBORDINATE FEMALE. Do you recognize the defendant?

ADOLESCENT MALE. Yeah, he's my dad.

SUBORDINATE FEMALE. Has he ever acted in a way that you feel is inappropriate for father figure or a leader?

ADOLESCENT MALE. Most of my life.

ALPHA MALE. Objection. My son is hardly worthy of giving an opinion about me, Your Honor. He can't even shake a man's hand right.

FIELD SCIENTIST. Is that true, son?

ADOLESCENT MALE. I don't know.

ALPHA MALE. My point.

FIELD SCIENTIST. Sustained. *(to* **SUBORDINATE FEMALE***)* You're dismissed.

ALPHA MALE. Can you give us an example of this supposed inappropriate behavior?

ADOLESCENT MALE. Once when I was little he caught me eating a cookie when I wasn't supposed to, and to punish me he made me eat all of them until I threw up. *(adding quickly)* Then he made me eat that.

ALPHA MALE. So I made you eat the scary cookies, huh? Answer me this, boy, did you ever sneak a cookie again?

ADOLESCENT MALE. No, sir.

ALPHA MALE. That taught you respect. You must show deference to those more powerful than you, or they will destroy you. My point, most people would call that effective parenting. I'm finished with this witness.

SUBORDINATE FEMALE. Redirect, Your Honor.

FIELD SCIENTIST. If you must.

SUBORDINATE FEMALE. Do you feel this prepared you in any way to become the alpha male your father wishes you to become?

ADOLESCENT MALE. No.

SUBORDINATE FEMALE. No further questions, Your Honor.

FIELD SCIENTIST. You may step down. Call your next witness.

SUBORDINATE FEMALE. I call the step-brother of the alpha male to the stand.

(**ADOLESCENT MALE** *leaves the witness stand to be replaced by* **SECOND BANANA.**)

SUBORDINATE FEMALE. Have you ever found your brother's behavior to be in any way lacking, from what you would deem an Alpha Male's conduct should be.

SECOND BANANA. Well, I do run his company for him. I don't believe he's been to work in over three months, and when he does appear, it is only to intimidate others.

SUBORDINATE FEMALE. Nothing further.

ALPHA MALE. Is the company doing well?

SECOND BANANA. Yes, but…

ALPHA MALE. Am I in charge of the company?

SECOND BANANA. Yes, but…

ALPHA MALE. So, so far we've proven that I effectively punished my child to avoid repeating undesirable behavior, and that my company is doing well.

SECOND BANANA. But I run it.

ALPHA MALE. Are you under me?

SECOND BANANA. Well yes, but...

ALPHA MALE. *(to* **SUBORDINATE FEMALE***)* Thank you. Brilliant, just brilliant. Next. You just set them up, and let me knock them down.

SUBORDINATE FEMALE. I call the favorite child of the alpha male, the adolescent female, to the stand as a hostile witness.

SUBORDINATE FEMALE. What are your feelings toward your father?

ADOLESCENT FEMALE. I love my father, and he loves me.

ALPHA MALE. That's right pumpkin.

ADOLESCENT FEMALE. And nothing you could ever say, would change the way I feel about Daddy. You're just bitter because I'm prettier, and he likes me better.

SUBORDINATE FEMALE. Will the court direct the witness to only answer the questions directed at her.

FIELD SCIENTIST. Blah, blah, whatever she said.

ADOLESCENT FEMALE. Everyone knows you're just a bitter old maid.

SUBORDINATE FEMALE. So, there's nothing that our father has ever done, that you would judge as being out of line. Say the physical reprimands he has made against the alpha female.

ADOLESCENT FEMALE. Mom never brings it up, I don't see why you have to.

SUBORDINATE FEMALE. What about my lineage?

ADOLESCENT FEMALE. I mean not to be rude, but she is just a servant. It's not like it affects me or anything, but ewww.

SUBORDINATE FEMALE. So there's no incident that I could come up with to make you change your mind about the alpha male.

ADOLESCENT FEMALE. I think I already answered that question.

SUBORDINATE FEMALE. What if I were to tell you that he killed the family dog when you were little?

ADOLESCENT MALE. Oh, that's a good one, I forgot about that.

ADOLESCENT FEMALE. You did what?

ALPHA MALE. The lesson was to teach obedience.

ADOLESCENT MALE. But he was a good dog.

ALPHA MALE. The lesson was for your brother, not for the dog.

ADOLESCENT FEMALE. You killed Fuzzy? You killed my Fuzzy?

ALPHA MALE. It was a lesson in obedience.

ADOLESCENT FEMALE. You killed my dog to teach my stupid brother a lesson? Oh my God, they were right. You are a bad man. I hate you.

ALPHA MALE. There is no good or bad. This is exactly why I didn't want you to take them to church when they were little. Fill their heads full of ideas. Good and bad, right and wrong. None of that matters. There is only survival of the fittest. You will all survive out there in that world. That world doesn't care about fair. It doesn't care if you were treated reasonably or not. If only cares about itself. You will endure. I have made sure of that.

SECOND BANANA. That's really sick, Jason. I think we've had enough of your survival of the fittest over the years.

FIELD SCIENTIST. Though to the group at large, these atrocities only confirm the dominance of the alpha male. His authority is never truly questioned, because they all fear his reprimand. They all fear him. They sometimes challenge, but they all pay the price. They feel confident in attempting to challenge him now, because they are in mass. Individually, none could stand up to him... sometimes it takes a village. Everyone has a weakness.

SUBORDINATE FEMALE. I now call the Alpha Female to the stand.

ALPHA FEMALE. *(She does not take the witness stand.)* We might as well forgo the pleasantries. This is where I am supposed to share with the court that my husband has had numerous affairs, which he will claim to be my fault. I should also share that he has felt the need to physically impose his will on me, that no doubt he felt he had the right to do, or can manipulate the situation to make it seem so. So why don't we forgo all this, Jason? Why don't you just answer some questions for us?

ALPHA MALE. You want me to take the witness stand?

FIELD SCIENTIST. This is highly irregular.

ALPHA MALE. And who's going to question me, you?

ALPHA FEMALE. I think this is Kate's area of expertise, why don't we let her continue.

ALPHA MALE. *(laughing)* In that case I would be more than happy to oblige.

(**ALPHA MALE** *takes the witness stand.*)

FIELD SCIENTIST. This is highly irregular. You can't just…

ALPHA MALE. I don't think we need you anymore. I can take it from here.

FIELD SCIENTIST. This is my courtroom. You can't just… You need me.

ALPHA MALE. I'm not accustomed to repeating myself. I said, I can handle it from here.

FIELD SCIENTIST. *(suddenly overly gracious)* Very well.

(**FIELD SCIENTIST** *and* **JANE** *slip back into their scientific roles.*)

ALPHA MALE. I wait with bated breath, what is your first question? Whatever will it be?

SUBORDINATE FEMALE. *(handing the* **ALPHA MALE** *papers)* Actually, I've got something for you. I hope you like it, I had them drawn up special for you.

ALPHA MALE. What the hell is this?

SUBORDINATE FEMALE. What does it look like? She finally listened to me.

ALPHA MALE. Divorce.

SUBORDINATE FEMALE. That's what it says at the top.

ALPHA MALE. Divorce, but we had an agreement.

ALPHA FEMALE. And I have suffered through that agreement through thick and thin, but enough is enough.

ALPHA MALE. If you do this I'll ruin you.

ALPHA FEMALE. I'm dying anyway. Really it takes the fear right out of me. Besides you'll get very little of what I have left.

ALPHA MALE. And who are you trusting to this monumental task. Our own dear sweet, Kate? You'll be killed in court. I'll get the best attorney your money can buy.

SUBORDINATE FEMALE. Actually, mom's already frozen the accounts under my advisement, so you won't be able to access funds quite so readily.

ALPHA MALE. I'm sure I can find someone to represent me better than you.

SUBORDINATE FEMALE. Actually, I won't be handling this case, I just helped draw up the papers. The head of our firm is coming out of semi-retirement to personally handle the case. He's heard so much about you, I think he just wants to meet you personally. I'm certain you won't disappoint, father.

FIELD SCIENTIST. This is a great big taboo. We don't get to see this very often in the field. The subordinate female is bringing in an outside alpha male to challenge her familial alpha male. The alpha male has really got to be feeling the pressure now.

ALPHA MALE. Why is it so hot in here?

(**ALPHA MALE** *is starting to get uncomfortable and begins to pull at his clothes.*)

ALPHA FEMALE. When I first met you Jason, I thought you were so dashing. Your manners were genteel, and he had obviously mastered elocution. It's the touch most men miss, but not you Jason. Elegant, well spoken, dapper. I was quite taken by you. A newlywed and a virgin, I learned some insights about my new husband.

OUTSIDE FEMALE. I thought I cared for your husband very much. I thought he cared for me.

ALPHA FEMALE. He does have that effect on people, doesn't he.

SUBORDINATE FEMALE. I was looking over the adoption paperwork, it's not really quite legal, it seems you owe Mary some eighteen years of back child support, I suppose that will come out of your portion as well.

ALPHA MALE. Did you do this?

ALPHA FEMALE. And you were just happy as a clam. Two women to serve you in two different ways. Financially and sexually.

ALPHA MALE. I don't need your money, anyway. I do have a job, you realize. It pays me quite well.

SECOND BANANA. Actually, you had a job.

ALPHA MALE. I beg your pardon.

SECOND BANANA. An outside investor bought the company last week, with your wife's financial support. You were found to be obsolete and replaced.

ALPHA MALE. By who.

SECOND BANANA. By me.

OUTSIDE MALE. Sad really.

ALPHA MALE. Shut up you little brown faggot. Did you do this?

ALPHA FEMALE. Do what?

ALPHA MALE. *(Speech builds to the end.)* Do what? Everyone was well provided for. Did you ever want for food or shelter? Did our children ever go without shoes? You were all well taken care of. Think of those people who have nothing. They would kill to have warm food in their belly, but you ungrateful wretches don't even understand what a great thing you've had. I brought you up to be strong, to be leaders. I was hard on you to make you strong. You will all survive this world because of me. You question me. How dare you question what I have given you.

FIELD SCIENTIST. *(aside)* The alpha male is being ambushed here from all sides. I'm not certain if it's even possible for him to reestablish his authority here. What's really surprising here is that the group has been daring enough to launch this attack. After all the years of being suppressed, it's truly shocking that they would even attempt this. This isn't even close to over, the alpha male is a true threat here. Remember, animals are most dangerous when they are wounded.

ALPHA MALE. *(now almost completely disheveled)* You can't do this to me. You don't have the right.

(picks up the penalty flag and throws it to the ground and pleads to **JANE***)*

FIELD SCIENTIST. This is not alpha male behavior right here. Throwing the penalty flag is definitely coming from some desperately devastated hole deep from inside the alpha male.

ALPHA MALE. I'm the man. I'm the only real man in this entire fucking family. No woman can put me in my place.

(The **ALPHA MALE** *launches himself at the* **ALPHA FEMALE***. He is more powerful than she is and starts to pin and beat her. He rips off some of her clothes. The* **ADOLESCENT MALE** *jumps him. Some of the* **ADOLESCENT MALE** *'s clothes get torn away. The* **ALPHA MALE** *throws him off easily.)*

FIELD SCIENTIST. Each blow, from the divorce to the loss of job and finances, has acted to wound the alpha male, but he is still stronger than any individual in the group. The alpha male is going to make one last stab at retaining his dominance.

ALPHA MALE. *(to* **ADOLESCENT FEMALE***)* It doesn't matter if I taught your mother a lesson or two over the years or killed your pathetically trusting dog, you would not have learned to survive on your own if it hadn't been for me. *(to* **SECOND BANANA***)* Who taught you how to fuck, boy? *(to* **SUBORDINATE FEMALE***)* Who put that fire in your belly, taught you how to hate everything

that wasn't right for you? *(to* **ADOLESCENT MALE***)* Hell,
I don't know what I taught you, boy, but imagine the
condition you'd be in if it weren't for me. Goddamn
mama's boy. *(to* **ALPHA FEMALE***)* You've always been irri-
tating, but you've never been stupid. I could kill you
where you stand.

ALPHA FEMALE. Try it.

(The **ALPHA MALE** *attacks the* **ALPHA FEMALE** *and all
the other characters begin disrobing and joining the fray,
as their chimpanzee counter parts. Though the* **ALPHA
MALE** *is easily killing the* **ALPHA FEMALE***, one by one
they circle and attack him. They jab here and there until
he is weak from being attacked from all sides.)*

FIELD SCIENTIST. The alpha male could easily defeat any of
his tribe one on one, but together they provide a powerful force for bringing down their leader. As a group
they must see a weakness in him that is not apparent
to all. A group never destroys a great leader, right? Of
course, mere animals have no concept of right and
wrong. They only sense that they want the strongest
leader for their group. If he cannot meet the challenges of the group, then he must be destroyed. For if
they do not destroy him, then surely someone else will.

(Suddenly they all rush in and attack the **ALPHA MALE**
*simultaneously. They attack him until he begins to con-
vulse. They all back away, watching him spasmodically
twitch. He slowly gets up to a seated position, with his
knuckles on the ground in front of him.)*

FIELD SCIENTIST. Through sheer force of will, the alpha
male is hanging onto life. Refusing to die. Trying to
regain his composure. Trying to merely survive. His
will is strong, but his body is weak, and it is beginning
to betray him.

*(***ALPHA MALE** *circles around trying to shake it off. The*
ALPHA MALE *staggers and then falls over. He reaches
out to find no one there. The* **ALPHA MALE** *dies. The
others slowly move in and begin to cautiously poke at the
body. After realizing he will not get back up they begin*

to celebrate and the **SECOND BANANA** *stands tall as the new* **ALPHA MALE** *as he removes the necklace that makes the* **ALPHA MALE** *the leader.)*

A new alpha male has risen to replace the old. A new leader to ensure his group's survival. He will maintain his position for as long as he can. He will remain the alpha male until he is found to be weaker than another male, and replaced by that male.

*(***SECOND BANANA*** takes the necklace and holds it high. He then places it over the head of the* **SUBORDINATE FEMALE**. **SECOND BANANA** *kneels before* **SUBORDINATE FEMALE***. The characters slowly follow and show respect for her, then they begin to parallel their movements as they did at the beginning of the play with the exception of the* **SUBORDINATE FEMALE** *who now watches over the entire clan.)*

This is simply unheard of. The new alpha male has had position as leader of their clan supplanted by the subordinate female, who appears to have taken position as the highest-ranking alpha member of the clan. This spells certain disaster for our clan. There is no way a mere woman could lead a mixed gender group successfully.

*(***JANE*** is clearly agitated by this.)*

No group could survive the leadership of a woman. This short-lived reign of the female will undoubtedly so render the demise of the group. If only the male had not relinquished his power, they might have been saved. But to think that a woman could be in a place of ultimate authority is not only impractical but dangerous, not only for her, but for those whom she would lead.

*(***JANE*** shoots the* **FIELD SCIENTIST** *with a dart. The* **ADOLESCENT MALE** *comes over and sniffs the* **FIELD SCIENTIST** *and then takes his tag off and places it on the* **FIELD SCIENTIST***. The* **ADOLESCENT MALE** *takes the clipboard up from where* **JANE** *has left it and begins to draw on it while watching the* **FIELD SCIENTIST***.)*

JANE. It is inevitable in the survival of any species that the group must adapt to change and grow as a community. Natural leadership abilities begin to show in certain individuals regardless of gender and social status. The only way to ensure survival is through evolutionary steps that will lead to an ever-evolving society. This is not a lesson in morality, but one of survival. Survival of the fittest.

(Time clock returns.)

Only time will tell.

(All the chimps have exited the stage except for four males and the **SUBORDINATE FEMALE***. As* **JANE** *exits, the four males form a live evolutionary scale with the* **SUBORDINATE FEMALE** *completing the image. Blackout.)*